THE FABULOUS BAKER BOYS

THE FABULOUS BAKER BOYS

The Greatest Strikers
Scotland Never Had

TOM MAXWELL

Foreword by
DENIS LAW

BIRLINN

First published in 2013 by
Birlinn Limited
West Newington House
10 Newington Road
Edinburgh
EH9 1QS

www.birlinn.co.uk

ISBN: 978 1 78027 174 3

British Library Cataloguing-in-Publication Data
A catalogue record for this book is available from the
British Library

For Jenna
It must be love

Typeset in Adobe Garamond at Birlinn

Printed and bound by
Gutenberg Press, Malta

Contents

Illustrations

Foreword
by Denis Law

The first time I ever pulled on a Scotland shirt, it was one of the proudest days of my life. So I can't imagine what it must have felt like for Joe Baker, a boy every bit as Scottish as me, when he was told he would never be able to do the same because he happened to be born in England. He was a terrific player and it would have been a pleasure to play alongside him in a dark-blue shirt at Hampden.

Instead, I played against him when he was making only his second appearance for England. It was hard to imagine a guy with his accent appearing in the same international line-up as the likes of Bobby Charlton and Jimmy Greaves, but that shows just how talented Joe was. Imagine a 19-year-old Hibs player being selected for England – it was unheard of then and it would be unheard of now.

While I was at Manchester City I played alongside Joe's older brother, Gerry. Not only was he a real character off the field, but he was lightning quick on it, a great goalscorer who also ended up playing international football – for the United States.

In 1961 I left Manchester City to sign for Torino at the same time as Joe – I couldn't get rid of the Baker boys! But, during that season, when the two of us had such trouble adjusting to playing football in Italy, I was very grateful for Joe's company. While in Italy, we were involved in a serious car crash. I escaped practically unscathed, but Joe suffered serious facial injuries and it says a lot for his determination and his courage that he was able to bounce back so quickly, continue his remarkable goalscoring at Arsenal and force his way back into the England team. Joe Baker was world-class no matter who he was playing for: Hibs, Torino, Arsenal . . . even England.

Denis Law, February 2013

Acknowledgements

The story of Joe and Gerry Baker, the Lanarkshire-bred footballing brothers who, through "accidents of birth", ended up representing England and the United States respectively, is unique – a story that deserved to be told. It was always important to me to have the wholehearted support of the Baker family and I was delighted when Gerry, as well as Joe's children Nadia and Colin, entrusted me with telling this remarkable tale. I hope this book makes them feel proud. Although I spent many hours trawling through old newspapers, reading historic match reports and researching in various libraries, it is the memories of former team-mates and opponents that have really brought the story of Gerry and Joe Baker to life and I am extremely grateful to the following for giving up their time to be interviewed or provide quotes for this book: Tony Allen, Frank Blunstone, Willie Carr, Sir Bobby Charlton, Roy Cheetham, David Court, Kenny Davidson, Dixie Deans, George Eastham, Fred Eyre, Paddy Fagan, Steve Fleet, Ron Flowers, John Fraser, Bob Gansler, Billy Hunter, Gordon Jago, Bobby Kinloch, Denis Law, Gordon Marshall, Ally Miller, Jim Montgomery, Doug Moran, Jimmy O'Rourke, Tom Preston, Alan Peacock, Sammy Reid, Lawrie Reilly, John Robertson, Jim Rodger, Willy Roy, Pat Stanton, Ian Storey-Moore, Dennis Tueart, Richard Williams, Bob Wilson and Alex Young.

I would also like to extend a big thank-you to the following for their help with contacts, facts and figures, photographs and various other bits of information that helped make *The Fabulous Baker Boys* possible: Deborah Benn, Mike Berry, Kerry Black, Jim Brown, Neil Buethe, Crystal Chesters, Tony Cirino, Iain Cook, Peter Creed, Maurice Dougan, Jim Douglas, Alex Edwards, Roddy Forsyth, Colin MacDonald, Willie McEwan, Dave Morrison, Simon Pryde, Phil Shaw, Jim Trecker, John Wilson, and the staff at the National Library of Scotland and Motherwell Heritage Centre. I would also like to thank my agent, David Fletcher, as well as Tom Johnstone and the team at Birlinn.

On a personal note, I want to thank my Mum and Dad for their love and support.

Prologue

"We ain't that bad, are we?"

The police sergeant sat and stared at the radio in silence. For the first time in his life, he was indecisive. Slowly, he replaced the handset and then looked across at his young colleague, who was waiting for his superior to give the word. Another moment passed before the silence was shattered.

"What the hell are you waiting for?" yelled the sergeant. "Step on it!" The constable didn't need to be told twice. Knocking the Panda into first gear, he gripped the steering wheel and pushed down hard on the accelerator. He felt his heart pounding as they began to race through the streets of north London. The constable had been involved in pursuits before, tailing criminals through Hackney, Lewisham and Brixton. But this assignment was making him feel particularly uneasy.

He didn't need to say anything. The sergeant clearly felt exactly the same way. It didn't matter how many horrible cases a police officer might have to work on during his career – burglaries, assaults, even murders – this was the one thing guaranteed to make even the most experienced copper nervous. After all, who in their right mind *would* want to come face to face with a mad Scotsman? The constable shuddered. He screeched round a corner and saw his quarry – a black cab.

"That's him," said the sergeant, double-checking the registration in his notebook. "Go for it." The constable took a deep breath and turned on the siren, signalling for the taxi to pull over. Both vehicles came to a halt in a layby. The front door of the taxi opened and the driver stepped out. He looked shaken. He signalled towards the back of his cab. He then tapped his temple with his forefinger – the universal sign to indicate that someone was off their rocker. As he had explained in hushed tones over the radio, he had picked up his passenger at London Airport and, almost immediately, the alarm bells had started to ring.

"Where to mate?" he had asked. "Hendon Hotel, please, pal," his passenger had replied. The accent was pure Scotch – thicker than the porridge the Jocks ate for breakfast. "The Hendon?" he said, setting the fare and pulling away from the airport. "That's where the England football team are staying."

"Aye, that's right," chirruped the stranger. "Ah'm playin' fer England at Wembley!" With those words, the conversation had died. The driver couldn't quite put his finger on it, but something about a man with a broad Scottish accent saying that he was playing for England just didn't add up.

His imagination began to run wild. Was this a spy? Someone sent to bring down English football from within? No, he thought. If that were the case, surely he'd have made more of an effort to disguise his tartan twang. Maybe his fare was just a piss-taking troublemaker, either that or he was completely out of his tree. Surreptitiously, the cabbie had radioed for assistance and now, much to his relief, the assistance had arrived.

The sergeant looked at the constable and nodded. Bracing himself, the constable opened the back door of the taxi. The lunatic was young. Probably only a teenager. He looked a bit like a film star. His dark hair was combed into an immaculate quiff, while his handsome features betrayed utter bewilderment.

"Good evening sir," said the constable. "Would you mind stepping out of the vehicle please?" The young man did as he was told, at which point the constable let his superior do the talking.

"So . . ." said the sergeant, looking the Scotsman up and down and barely able to believe the words he was about to utter, "you're playing for England, are you, sonny?"

"Aye, that's right," spluttered the youngster. "Ah'm playin fer England on Wednesday night!"

The sergeant stared at him, his expression blank. The young man corrected himself. "Ahem, Ah mean, *yes*. I'm playing for England."

The sergeant sighed. "Do you have any ID, young man? Any identification?"

The young man reached into the pocket of his overcoat and, after several seconds of fumbling, produced his passport, along with a newspaper. He handed both over to the police officer and pointed to the back page of the paper. "Latest edition," he said.

The sergeant, more baffled than ever, took the newspaper and began to read about the England football team's new centre-forward – a teenager who had never played the game outside of Scotland. He then looked at the photograph accompanying the article. "That's me," said the young Scot, tapping the picture with more than a hint of pride in his voice.

"Nineteen-year-old Joe Baker," read the sergeant, "is one of the top goal-scorers in Scottish football. Pictured in the colours of Hibernian, he will earn his first full cap for England against the Irish on Wednesday night."

"*Hibernian?*" thought the sergeant. "*Where the hell's that?*" His musings were interrupted by his junior colleague, who had been studying the article over his shoulder.

"Jesus Christ, Sarge!" he exclaimed. "A Jock playing for England? Surely we ain't that bad, are we?"

1
Birth-wrong

"Being born in a stable does not make one a horse." This was how Daniel O'Connell, the former Lord Mayor of Dublin, reportedly commented on the nationality of the Irish-born Duke of Wellington. It is unlikely, however, that such an argument would have held much sway with The Four British Associations, the committee charged with setting eligibility criteria for Home Nations footballers, for Joe Baker.

Had the prolific Hibernian striker, in a Lanarkshire accent so broad that even his Edinburgh team-mates had difficulty understanding him, suggested to the committee that being born in Liverpool did not make him an Englishman, it would have fallen on profoundly deaf ears. Being born in an English city, even if it was his home for all of six weeks, was enough to make Joe, in the eyes of the committee, as English as Billy Wright or Bill Shakespeare.

While he may at times have viewed the circumstances of his birth as a cruel twist of fate, it also gave Joe the opportunity to become a unique fixture in the oldest rivalry of them all. The matches between England and Scotland are as fiercely contested today as they were when the nations first met in Partick back in 1872, with historic mutual antagonism rearing its ugly head on each occasion. The existence of the Union may have prevented all-out war, but football at least gives the protagonists the chance to boot each other around the pitch every once in a while.

It would be hard to argue, however, with the assertion that the rivalry is more keenly felt by the smaller of the two nations. Any Englishman who has his doubts should try watching *Braveheart* in a cinema full of Scots. Joe Baker, in the words of former Scotland Schoolboys team-mate Sammy Reid, "was just as Scottish as the rest of us". Yet although he lived only 15 miles from Hampden Park, the rules of 1959 dictated that the 19-year-old could play only for the country in which he was born – affinity, pride and a preference for mince and tatties over liver and onions didn't come into it. As a wide-eyed teenager with film-star looks and the world at his feet, he was prepared to play international football for anybody – even if it was for the so-called "Auld Enemy".

Those who doubted his commitment to the English cause only needed to watch his full-blooded shoulder charge on Scotland goalkeeper Frank

Haffey at Hampden in 1960. Years later, when the boots had been hung up and the selectors had stopped watching, the man who played for England under both Walter Winterbottom and Alf Ramsey declared: "The only thing that bothers me is that I wasn't born in Scotland." It bothered Denis Law too, the legendary No 10 admitting: "Joe Baker wouldn't have been good for Scotland – he would have been great."

Law, together with legions of success-starved Scotland supporters, can only wonder what might have been. Had Joe's mother decided to move north of the Border six weeks earlier, he would surely have had the chance to make many more appearances in the dark blue of Scotland, building a legend that might have challenged that even of Law himself.

Instead, Joe became the answer to a perennial pub quiz favourite – the man who wore the Three Lions but spoke with a Scottish accent. Aside from the adoring, but ageing, fans who watched him grace the likes of Easter Road, Highbury and Nottingham Forest's City Ground, he is a footnote in the annals of England's national football team. Were eight caps really just reward for a player of such precocious talent? A man who, after scoring 100 goals for Hibs before he was 21, went on to reach a century for Arsenal quicker than the likes of Thierry Henry, Cliff Bastin and Robin van Persie? Joe Baker played his last game for England in January 1966, when he appeared alongside the same group of footballers whose Wembley heroics would still be eulogised by the English media nearly half a century on. But would the same media be quite so vocal about the World Cup win had it been Joe Baker, rather than Geoff Hurst, who scored the hat-trick against West Germany?

Over the years, the Tartan Army, the collective name of Scotland's die-hard supporters, has grown accustomed to the sight of "Englishmen" playing for Scotland. These "Englishmen" include Stuart McCall, Andy Goram and Don Hutchison, the Geordie whose winner at Wembley had England scrabbling to qualify for Euro 2000 by the skin of their teeth. Scots are happy to forgive a player his birthplace, so long as he gives everything for his adoptive homeland.

A Scotsman prepared to pull on a shirt bearing the Three Lions crest, however, was another matter entirely. Long after the boos and the calls of "ya Sassenach" had rained down on him from the Hampden terracing, Joe Baker still found himself on the receiving end of taunts – some friendly, some less so.

But while playing for Scotland was never an option for Joe, his older brother, Gerry, signed away his chance to play for the country he called home. Despite having a Lanarkshire accent every bit as strong as his younger brother's, the man who scored in every round of St Mirren's Scottish Cup victory of 1959 was born in the United States, something that earned him the nickname, "The Yank of Love Street".

He had made a conscious decision, actually one at the request of his mother, to sign his US citizenship papers when he turned 21. While it may have allowed him to avoid National Service, declaring himself a son of the Stars and Stripes meant that Gerry would have to wait until his best years were behind him before he got his first taste of international football. That one stroke of the pen did, however, give Gerry his own unique claims to fame. After becoming the first "American" to score a hat-trick in the English First Division, he became, at the age of 30, the first top-flight European player to represent the planet's most powerful nation as it took its baby steps into the world of soccer. Like Joe, Gerry scored goals at international level. But that was no great surprise.

In combined careers that included spells at Chelsea, Hibs, Arsenal, Torino, Motherwell, St Mirren, Coventry City, Nottingham Forest, Ipswich Town and Sunderland, the Baker brothers scored more than 500 professional goals. Gerry and Joe even scored ten and nine goals in respective Scottish Cup matches. Impressive statistics, but it is their appearances on the international scene that make the siblings' story stand apart.

A total of 15 caps between them may not sound huge, especially in an era when footballing priorities have changed, but the Bakers played football in an age when pulling on the colours of their country was considered the ultimate honour. Today, many of the game's highly paid professionals regard an international as just one more match in an increasingly crowded diary of fixtures. With the UEFA Champions League glorified as the ultimate feast of football, it is little wonder that the international game has not so much taken a back seat, but been booted out of the car altogether.

A combination of the FIFA World Cup now welcoming 32 competitor nations and international friendlies now allowing up to 11 substitutions per match has resulted in caps being dished out like confetti. At this juncture, members of the jury should turn their attention to Exhibit A: Phil Neville, and Exhibit B: Emile Heskey, who between them managed to amass 121 international appearances for England. Had Joe Baker, a man revered by players such as Denis Law, Bobby Charlton and Lawrie Reilly, been plying his trade today, he might have reached that total on his own.

And while Joe, in the words of his brother, would have given his right arm to play for Scotland, today's footballers can virtually choose their nationality at will. Since Joe's call-up to senior England duty in 1959, the goalposts of international eligibility have moved on several occasions. Once as strict as passport control, selection criteria are now as rigid as a house

3

of cards. Look at the German-born Boateng brothers, for example. While Jerome represents the land of his birth, his brother, Kevin Prince, elected to play for Ghana. And the global melting pot of modern-day football has seen international avenues opening up for some of the least likely players. Former Wimbledon midfielder Robbie Earle could never have imagined that, one day, he would score for Jamaica in the World Cup finals. And not even the most fanciful of Hollywood directors would have dreamt of casting Vinnie Jones as the captain of the Welsh national football team.

While a Liverpool birth was enough to restrict Joe Baker to an international career with England, Chesterfield-born Bob Wilson was able to use his father's birth certificate to gain two caps for Scotland in 1971. Several years later, Jack Charlton utilised the "Granny Rule" to great effect when a Republic of Ireland side containing a healthy smattering of Cockneys, Scousers and Yorkshiremen reached the quarter-finals of the 1990 World Cup.

Twenty-first century players find many ways to work their way into international reckoning, whether it's by means of education, citizenship or even marriage. If that fails, they can use some of their vast wealth to employ genealogists from *Who Do You Think You Are?* in the hope that a long-dead ancestor will provide them with the key to playing for a nation of their choice. Or maybe they'll take comedy actor Ralph Little's route into international football and write to the Principality of Sealand, the North Sea defence platform which claims sovereign status.

For Joe and Gerry Baker, however, playing international football was no joke. It was something of which they were very proud – regardless of the countries they represented. Although, today, the respective playing careers of the Baker brothers are fondly remembered, both were nearly over before they had the chance to begin.

2
Finishing School

New Rochelle, so the song goes, is just 45 minutes from Broadway. And, for George and Elizabeth Baker, the city where Don McLean would one day write *American Pie* was a million miles from their respective birthplaces of Liverpool and Motherwell. With George working as a door-to-door salesman and Lizzie earning money as a cleaner, the pair had met and married in the United States. Their pleasant home in upstate New York was the ideal place for the young British immigrants to raise a family, and it was here that their first child, Gerard Austin Baker, was born on 11 April 1938.

It is probably safe to assume that, when Mr and Mrs Baker became parents, the future footballing allegiances of their offspring weren't foremost in their minds. They could not know that, in 30 years' time, in the twilight of a successful career as a professional footballer, young Gerry would return to represent the land of his birth on the international soccer stage.

Years later, when Gerry was hoping to represent Scotland, he would lament his parents' sense of timing. It was a pattern he'd already noticed when he first heard one of his father's favourite stories about his time in New York. A keen sports fan, George had tried for several weeks to get a ticket to see heavyweight champion Joe Louis fight John Henry Lewis at Madison Square Garden on 25 January 1939. But, by the time George had parked his car and made his way to his seat, Lewis was sprawled on the canvas – the "Bum of the Month" being no match for the Brown Bomber.

Later that year, however, sport was the last thing on George's mind. With war having broken out in Europe, the Englishman felt he couldn't stand back and watch. All four of his brothers were serving in the British Navy. In America, he was helpless, so George, too, decided to join up, relocating his family from the north-east of the United States to the northwest of England. He returned to Liverpool, settling in Woolton Village, and the couple's second son, Joseph Henry, was born in Smithdown Road Infirmary on 17 July 1940. Exactly three months earlier, in the same hospital, a woman named Jean Wycherley gave birth to a son, Ronald. As Billy Fury, Ronald Wycherley would become a household name, but Joe Baker would become famous in his own right – as one of the deadliest finishers British football has ever seen.

But as many Liverpudlians would discover, wartime Merseyside wasn't safe. As a key port and gateway to the Atlantic, Liverpool, after London, became the prime target for the Luftwaffe. On the night of Wednesday, 28 August 1940, exactly six weeks after Joe's birth, 160 German bombers descended on the city. It was the beginning of the Liverpool Blitz. The unrelenting assault would eventually cost the lives of more than 4,000 residents, but Lizzie was determined that her two young sons would not be among the victims.

"We were basically bombed out of Liverpool," explains Gerry. "We were quite settled there, living with my dad's mother, but we weren't far from the Speke Aerodrome (now Liverpool John Lennon Airport) and my family used to hear the Ack-Ack guns firing at night, really blasting. It got worse and worse. The chip shop near our home was hit hard, so my mother decided that she was coming back to Scotland. She took Joe and me back to Wishaw, just outside Motherwell, to stay at my grandmother McShane's house while our dad continued to fight in the War."

Situated around ten miles from Glasgow, which would suffer heavy civilian losses of its own during the Clydebank Blitz of 1941, the town of Motherwell lay in the heart of industrial Lanarkshire. It was home to David Colville and Sons – the biggest steelworks in Britain, and, with the arrival of the Ravenscraig Steelworks in the 1950s, the town earned the nickname Steelopolis.

At the age of just two-and-a-half, Gerry Baker had already lived in three countries across two continents, but Motherwell was somewhere that he and his younger brother could finally call home. This would be the town in which the young Baker boys would fall in love with football, meeting some of the most influential people in the game. It was also where they would both be confronted with the kind of obstacles that would make any kind of career in professional sport seem unlikely – even impossible.

When he was three, Joe was struck down by tuberculosis and spent more than a year in hospital in Glasgow. "It was a killer," says Gerry. "He slept outside most of the time because it helped him to breathe. It was a miracle he survived to be four years old, let alone grow up to be a footballer."

Even at such a tender age, Joe demonstrated a great fighting spirit. After 18 months, he had beaten TB. He had faced incredible odds and won – and it wouldn't be the last time.

Like so many boys of that age during the War, the Baker brothers yearned for adventure and excitement. In 1944, their mother took them to the cinema to see a film called *The Fighting Sullivans* – a biopic of the five American brothers who were killed while serving aboard the same ship in the US Navy. What they didn't realise was that the story would soon seem very close to home.

"While we were watching the movie, a message flashed across the screen asking my mum to report to the foyer. That was when we learned that my dad's ship had been blown up," explains Gerry. "It was making its way back across the English Channel, but the irony was that it was a British mine that blew it up. My father was one of the only survivors. He got a piece of shrapnel in his stomach. He was landed at Portsmouth, they moved him to Middlesbrough, then we got him to Victoria Hospital in Glasgow. He was in and out of there for the next few years, before he finally succumbed to his wounds. He'd lost his bladder and he had no control, but he was able to keep going for about four years.

"When he was in a really bad way, he would have to get a taxi to the hospital in the middle of the night. We had moved into a pre-fab by this time. We didn't have a phone, so I would have to run from our house, across the railway line at Craigneuk and get a taxi from there to take him to hospital."

In many ways, it was remarkable that Gerry had been able to make the midnight dashes to aid his father. At the age of six, his own life was almost ended by the very mode of transport that helped to prolong his father's. "I can't really remember what happened," he says. "We always used to go with our granddad to collect milk at a smallholding. I think I was chasing the cows out when I ran the wrong side of a lorry and this taxi smacked into me. My right thigh was fractured and I was in hospital for over six months.

"When I went back to school I was like limp-a-long. When I was eight, I was playing football in the schoolyard and I managed to break the same leg again. There was no ambulance available so they brought me home in the next best thing – a hearse! There it was, parked outside my house, with me lying in the back. All the kids in the housing scheme came to see me and I was just lying there, giving them the thumbs-up. My mother was coming home from the shops when a neighbour came up to her, pointed to the hearse and said: 'It's your Gerry.' She collapsed in shock, and no wonder."

At one time, Lizzie Baker was doing the visiting rounds at three different hospitals. "It was unbelievable," admits Gerry, who adds that infections weren't the only thing you could pick up on a ward in Glasgow. "All the kids in there swore like troopers," he laughs. "When I got back home and my mum asked me to go and buy milk, I'd be like, 'fuck off mum!' *Wallop!* I remember the doctor saying to me that, after the second break, I'd never be able to play football, but I ended up being the fastest runner at every club I played for. Between crossing that railway line and running away from my mum, I had to be fast. Throughout my playing career, my right leg was quarter of an inch shorter than my left – and it still is!"

While survival instincts forced them to run from their mother, neither Gerry nor Joe ran away from fights in the school playground. "When we started attending Park Street Primary in Motherwell, the other kids were all looking at Joe and me like we were the Odd Couple," says Gerry. "We used to get a lot of stuff sent over from America: trousers with elastic bottoms or jackets with pleats, and Joe once went into school wearing some kind of blouse. We were wide open to the bullies, especially with one of us being born in England and the other being born in America. There was also the fact that both of us, through being in hospital and so on, were late coming into school. We missed out on a lot of our education. We were joining classes and didn't really know what the teachers were talking about. On the playground, we were fighting with other kids all the time. We had to learn to use our fists or they would really take advantage of us. Joe was tough. We had to be because we were getting into fights what seemed like every other day. We came to expect it."

The brothers honed their fighting skills at a local boxing club at Lanarkshire Welfare, with the younger sibling, despite his short stature, displaying more of a natural aptitude for the sport. "We used to go sparring at night when we had nothing else to do," says Gerry. "Lads would often either do that or play football. On one occasion Joe knocked me out cold. I obviously wasn't looking at the time! Chic Calderwood, who was a year older than me, came from Craigneuk, which is part of Wishaw. He became the British light-heavyweight champion, but Joe could have been middleweight champion of the world. If Joe hit you, you went down."

This was something that Liverpool giant Ron Yeats would discover, much to the hilarity of Joe's team-mates if not to the crowd, on the pitch at Anfield a number of years later. But while the Baker brothers enjoyed boxing, Gerry's real passion was the other great working-class escape: football. As he explained at the height of his fame with Hibs, however, Joe wasn't so keen at first.

"Gerry was crazy about football," he said. "Often, I couldn't have cared less. But it was Gerry who talked and coaxed me out to play, and made me as keen as himself. I don't think I'd have had all the breaks that have come to me in football if it wasn't for Gerry."

His brother says: "Hard as it is to imagine, Joe often wanted to play in goal. We'd play in these matches – about 20-a-side – on a field near our house in Range Road. We'd turn round and find that our goalkeeper, and our goalposts, had disappeared because he had grabbed his jumper and coat and was away home for his dinner! He started to play up front at school, and the lads – the bullies – all got used to us. We didn't have any boots or anything. We played in gutties [plimsolls]. We'd play at school, up in the field or in the street and, although we were the best players in the housing scheme, we never dreamt that we could ever be professionals."

When her boys became household names, Lizzie Baker spoke to a local newspaper about their childhood. "They've both been playing football since they were about eight, but all the boys in Motherwell kick footballs about, so I thought nothing of that," she said. "I thought they'd just grow up to be ordinary working men – nothing out of the ordinary if you know what I mean. Their school reports showed that they weren't stupid, but they weren't brainy either. One time, the headmaster wrote on Joe's report, 'I think Joe's brains have all fallen to his feet!'"

In terms of organised matches, the pair's first experience was with Park Street Primary, while they also turned out for Craigneuk Boys' Guild. "We were always first pick," says Gerry. "Neither of us wanted to play anywhere but up front. Joe was always scoring but we weren't competitive, at least not with each other. We fought together and we played together. We were like twins."

Joe recalled: "Sometimes I'd be at outside-right and Gerry would be at centre. Then it would be the other way around. We must have been a bit crazy about football. We played for the school on Saturday mornings, gulped down our dinner and dashed off to play for the Boys' Guild in the afternoon."

The brothers' goalscoring prowess soon became apparent. Gerry says: "We were playing for Craigneuk Boys' Guild against Cleland and beat them about 15-0. The two of us scored seven and a half goals each. Both of us went for our eighth goal and slid the ball over the line at the same time."

Lizzie said: "Joe would come home and tell me about all the goals he had scored – but I thought it was just his imagination." Joe's final year at Park St Primary saw him score more than 100 goals, including a hat-trick in the 3-0 win over Morningside Primary in the final of the Summer Cup, and win four trophies. While the effortless goalscoring was something he would repeat throughout his professional career, senior trophies would remain frustratingly elusive. At nine, Joe was the youngest member of the Motherwell and Wishaw Select side that won the Scottish Primary Schools Cup, beating an Aberdeen side, featuring a young Denis Law, in the final.

Former Motherwell inside-right Sammy Reid, Bill Shankly's first signing for Liverpool, grew up in Craigneuk. When he first played alongside Joe for the Motherwell and Wishaw Select side, he knew that his team-mate was no ordinary player. "Because I played with him and against him from when we were boys of nine and ten, as an experienced footballer, I have to say that he was the best I ever saw or ever played with. He wasn't the greatest player in a skilful sense but, by crikey, he was some goalscorer, and he was so quick. I played with a lot of good players and against a lot of good players, but I would put Joe Baker as No. 1 – above everybody."

Reid also played alongside Joe when, having moved to St Joseph's Secondary School, the latter was called up to represent his country – at least the one with which he most identified – in 1955. Although all four Home Nations now take part in the Victory Shield, an international competition for Under-15s, at the time only boys from England, Scotland and Wales competed.

Joe made his debut for Scotland Schoolboys against Wales in front of 7,000 supporters at Somerset Park, home of Ayr United, on Saturday, 7 May 1955. His first goal in international colours put Scotland 3-1 ahead shortly before half-time, in a match that saw the home side win comfortably 5-2.

The English-born striker found himself in good company. Also in the Scotland side was Willie Stevenson, an integral part of Bill Shankly's Anfield Revolution who won two league championships and an FA Cup with Liverpool, and Billy Cook, whose career with Melbourne side Slavia eventually saw him pick up seven full caps for Australia. Joe's second and final appearance in dark blue took place a week later, and involved a return to the city of his birth as Scotland travelled south to face their English counterparts at Goodison Park. With England having beaten Wales 6-2, only a win would be enough for Scotland to claim the Victory Shield. But with the home side having won the trophy five years in a row, Scotland began the match as underdogs.

Sure enough, they fell behind to an early goal, only for Joe to score twice in two minutes – the second a bullet-header – to give the young Scots a 2-1 half-time lead. Although England equalised in the second half, retaining the Victory Shield in the process, Joe's brace in front of a remarkable crowd of nearly 40,000 showed that he was more than capable of performing on the big occasion. His two goals against England is something Joe later admitted he would have loved to emulate at senior level, but he learned soon afterwards that this was an impossible dream.

The organisers of the Victory Shield, the Schools' International Board, stated in their rules that: "There shall be no birth qualification, but a boy shall have played football for, and be attending a school which is affiliated to the national association of, and in the country he represents." Unfortunately for Joe, the full national side's criteria were considerably more strict.

"I'll never forget the day I found out I would never be able to wear the dark blue jersey in a full international," he said. "I was just 15 and still at St Joseph's. One day, near the end of term, we were discussing what we wanted to do when we left school. I said I wanted to be a professional footballer, and added: 'And one day I'll play for Scotland.' That was when the rug was pulled out. My teacher explained: 'That you'll never do, Joe – you were born in England, so you cannot play for Scotland."

With the thought of one day turning out for England never entering his head, young Joe would have to content himself with the ambition of playing club football and, although Motherwell were his local team, there was only one side that truly captured his imagination.

Gordon Smith, Bobby Johnstone, Lawrie Reilly, Eddie Turnbull and Willie Ormond – collectively known as Hibs' Famous Five – were the most celebrated forward line in Scottish football, with most or all playing in the Edinburgh club's league championship wins of 1948, 1951 and 1952. In the 1955-56 season, Hibs became the first British side to compete in the newly formed European Cup, reaching the semi-finals. The quintet were all Scottish internationals, with Reilly behind only Denis Law, Kenny Dalglish and Hughie Gallacher on the all-time top-scorers list. Such is the Famous Five's legendary status that, in 2005, the North Stand at Easter Road was re-named in their honour. It was hardly surprising, then, that a trip to Fir Park to see the Famous Five in action made an indelible imprint on the minds of Joe and Gerry Baker.

"I can remember the day Joe decided he was a Hibs fan as though it were yesterday," says Gerry. "I was 14, Joe was 12. It was piddling rain and we were right down at the front. Hibs beat Motherwell 7-3 and the Famous Five, actually the Famous Four because Willie Ormond was injured, were magic. I had never seen Joe like that – he was utterly mesmerised and I just knew that something had clicked with him. We could never have imagined that we'd both end up playing for Hibs one day."

Joe admitted that, "Even as a child, I had a notion for Hibs," adding, "I didn't see much First Division football, but when Hibs came through to play Motherwell, I usually managed to be there. The sight of that famous Hibs forward line, and particularly of Lawrie Reilly, really did things to me. I don't think I've ever been aware of copying anyone, but if I have done it unconsciously, that player must be Lawrie Reilly."

Just five years after first marvelling at his brilliance as a child, Joe got the chance to play alongside Reilly for Hibs. In the intervening years, however, the goalscoring exploits of Gerry and Joe Baker managed to attract the attention of another club. This time, it was the champions of England who came calling.

3
Bridge of Sighs

If ever there was a man well placed to assess the quality of a young striker, it was Ted Drake. In 1935, the former Arsenal and England forward gave a new definition to clinical when he scored seven goals in a First Division match against Aston Villa – a top-flight record that still stands. When injury curtailed his prolific playing career, he turned his hand to management, joining Chelsea from Reading in 1952. And it wasn't long before Drake, who was only 40, began the process of dragging the club into the modern era. He brought a tougher, more ball-focused, ethos to the Stamford Bridge training ground. He even ditched the Chelsea Pensioner crest, overseeing its transformation to the lion sported by the players of Stamford Bridge today.

And with a philosophy of signing promising youngsters, including future England manager Ron Greenwood from Brentford and defender Derek Saunders from amateur side Walthamstow Avenue, "Drake's Ducklings" won Chelsea's first league championship in 1954-55. Blues supporters would have to wait more than half a century, with the arrival of a Portuguese Special One backed by a Russian billionaire, before they experienced similar joy.

Like Jose Mourinho, Drake was not content to rest on his laurels of winning a lone league title. His scouts continued to scour the UK, including Scotland, searching for fresh talent. They found it at Gasworks Park – home of Larkhall Thistle. The Jags line-up had often proved a happy hunting ground for top clubs, with future Scotland captains Jimmy Carabine, John Hutton, Andy McLaren, Willie McStay and Alex Raisbeck all having turned out for the country's oldest Junior football team. And it was here that Drake's right-hand men uncovered a lean – and frighteningly quick – 16-year-old with an eye for goal. He was also eager to succeed. On the face of it, Gerry Baker was the perfect fit for Chelsea.

"I finished school and went straight into work," says Gerry. "I signed for Larkhall and I enjoyed it, but the only problem was that there was a bit of a religious divide. The Bakers were Catholic, but I just told everyone I was Jewish! I only played two games for Larkhall when a chap from Middlesbrough came up to see me. My uncle Gerry, who was an ex-junior footballer, decided that Joe and I should both go down to Ayresome Park for a trial. Middlesbrough offered me terms but I didn't like the place so we came back. Joe was only 14 at this time. I played a few more games for Larkhall and then Chelsea came calling."

London seemed a long way away, particularly for a teenager, so Gerry asked Joe, and their uncle, to join him as he headed to the capital for a trial match. Stepping off the train at 6am, they got a taxi to Stamford Bridge, where they had to wait until the gates were opened at 9am. An hour later, Drake assembled the youngsters for the match at a nearby park. However, realising that he was a player short, Joe was thrown a pair of boots and asked to do his best. It seems that the fatigue of the journey had little effect on the brothers, with Gerry scoring twice and Joe getting a hat-trick. Both went home happy, and were persuaded to head south once more when Drake himself visited their home in Wishaw.

"It was only a few days after my 17th birthday," says Gerry. "And for Ted Drake, a lovely guy and probably one of the greatest goalscorers of all time, to come to see us in our own home and ask us to join Chelsea was a real thrill. I thought London would be great. Ted really liked Joe as well, but he hadn't even turned 15 at that stage. He was just a baby, really, and my mum felt he should finish school up in Scotland before moving. Besides, I think even then he knew he would be a Hibee."

It was agreed, however, that Joe would accompany Gerry in London for the summer holidays as he acclimatised to life as a young footballer in a bustling metropolis. "I was so excited when I played my first training match," he recalls. "I went tearing after the ball and crashed into Chic Thompson, the first-team goalkeeper. He called me an idiot, but it was just the excitement of thinking I was actually playing with Chelsea."

Joe, meanwhile, was getting a taste of life on the club's ground staff. Frank Blunstone, who won the league championship with Chelsea while doing his National Service, admits the ground staff role – which he had fulfilled while at Crewe – wasn't the most glamorous. "You'd wash the terraces, clean the dressing room, clean the boots of the pros – any bloody job that needed to be done, you had to do it," he says. "The ground staff at Chelsea weren't allowed to train with the pros."

But it wasn't just the menial tasks that got Joe down. "The digs were an absolute dump," says Gerry. "I remember Joe sitting there saying 'I want my mammy. I want to go home.' I loved London, but it can be a lonely place, especially for a 17-year-old."

Desperate to succeed, however, Gerry wasn't quite ready to follow his younger brother back to Scotland. Throughout the 1955-56 season, he played a mixture of youth and third-team matches for the Blues. Clearly making progress, the following season he made six appearances for the reserves, scoring four goals. Even competition for a place in the second-string side, who attracted crowds of around 5,000 at Stamford Bridge, proved tough for Gerry.

"The reserves were of a very high standard," explains Blunstone. "They would alternate with the first team playing at home. They played in the London Combination, which included West Ham and Arsenal."

And such was the quality of the forward line in Chelsea's youth ranks that Gerry was pushed out to the wing, where he went from goal-scorer to goal-provider, and, more often than not, it was the same young man that enjoyed the benefit. Gerry says: "To tell you the truth, I only had one job for the Chelsea youth team: crossing the ball to Jimmy Greaves and clapping him on the back, saying, 'Well done, Jimmy, that's another great goal!'"

Eventually, however, Gerry was given his big chance. On 26 September 1956, he was selected for a mid-week Southern Professional Floodlit Cup match away to Luton Town. The competition, a straight knockout and a precursor to the League Cup (in all its various sponsorship guises), was hardly at the top of Drake's priority list. Nevertheless, it gave Gerry, who had been providing the peerless Greaves with plenty of assists, a chance to show what he could do.

"What a moment, to be picked for the first team," he says. "I even had my picture in the newspaper – I thought, 'Ooh, I'm famous!' But I was terrible. I don't know what happened but I didn't do well. I was playing at outside right, I was a flying machine, but I didn't do myself justice at all. It was a fantastic experience, playing alongside the likes of Roy Bentley, Johnny McNichol and Frank Blunstone, but I was back in the youth team the very next game. It knocked the stuffing out of me."

Chelsea lost the match 4-2 to Luton, the eventual winners of the trophy. When it became obvious that a second call-up to the first team probably wouldn't be coming his way any time soon, Gerry decided he'd had enough. "We were on the bus, coming back from a youth team game," he recalls. "Jimmy had been banging in the goals, as usual, and he asked me if I fancied going to the pictures. I said no and that I was going home. But I didn't mean going back to the digs, I meant going back to Scotland. I spent that night packing my bags and the next morning I headed for the train station. I was walking down the street and whom should I meet, of all people, but Ted Drake. He said hello and asked me where I was off to. Thinking quickly, I told him I was taking my clothes to the laundrette, but that was me gone. I got on the train and never went back."

Blunstone says: "Gerry was unlucky because he didn't quite make it to the top at Chelsea. But it was incredibly difficult because we had about 47 pros on the books at Stamford Bridge in those days, so Gerry had an awful lot of competition." In stark contrast to the Chelsea squad of today, Gerry was the only member of the club's entire playing staff to be born outside of the UK and Ireland.

On learning that the young striker, far from taking his pants to be washed, had actually done a runner, Drake said he was "very disappointed Baker should have walked out like this," adding, "He is a promising young player." The manager then proceeded to hit Gerry with a six-month suspension. This gave the teenager plenty of time to think, with the question of which club would want him now at the forefront of his mind. Joe, on the other hand, knew there was only one team he wanted to play for.

4
Easter Comes Early

In 1955, the task of unearthing exciting new players at Easter Road fell to Davie Wyper, Hibs' chief scout. While Hibs' Famous Five-inspired side had won the league championship three times in the late Forties and early Fifties, the club could not continue to rely on the combined brilliance of Johnstone, Ormond, Reilly, Smith and Turnbull. Johnstone had just been sold to Manchester City and, sooner or later, replacements – if such players existed – for the others would also need to be found. Wyper could, however, enjoy the luxury of football's maximum wage, which meant that even clubs the size of Hibs could offer meagre terms to a veritable army of youngsters. If things didn't work out, the young player could be let go, with no real harm done to the club's finances.

Doug Moran, who was at Easter Road from the age of 16, left at 21 having made only a handful of first-team appearances. The inside-forward, who went on to score more than 100 goals for Falkirk and won the English First Division with Alf Ramsey's Ipswich Town in 1962, found the Edinburgh club's tendency to bring in so many players a real stumbling block. "They had about 50 staff on the books at that time," he recalls. "They kept signing people every week. Every time you went into the ground there would be another three players that you didn't recognise."

With a potential cast of hundreds lining up to appear on the Easter Road stage, it was a question of who would be the primary players, who would be among the chorus and who would be forever waiting in the wings. In 1955, one of the players Moran spotted in training was Joe Baker – a teenager from Lanarkshire who Moran, and the rest of the country, would soon come to recognise as a precocious talent. Already a Scotland Schoolboy international, Joe had initially been spotted by Wyper while playing for St Joseph's Secondary School in Motherwell and, after returning from his brief stay in London, he was quickly offered provisional terms with his favourite club.

To ensure he had plenty of playing time, Hibs farmed out their promising new centre forward to the now defunct Wishaw club, Coltness United. On 12 September, 1955, Joe made a spectacular debut for Hibernian A at Easter Road. Following his four goals in the 10-1 victory over Armadale

Thistle, a local newspaper reported: "Hibs look to have a really great player in the making. Time will tell."

Time did tell. While at Coltness, Joe managed to score 40 goals and, on 6 May 1956, he became the youngest ever player to feature for the Lanarkshire Select, when they met the Leinster Senior League. After leaving school and beginning an apprenticeship at Pickering's steelworks as a welder, Joe spent the following season, 1956-57, at Armadale Thistle, another Hibs feeder club. According to winger Johnny MacLeod, who later played alongside Joe at Easter Road and then at Highbury, the pair were moved out to West Lothian for a bit of "toughening up". It didn't do either player any harm, with Joe scoring 52 goals, a feat that had a number of supporters comparing him to the great Lawrie Reilly. He would get his chance, they claimed, to emulate his hero in a Hibs shirt, but fate would present that chance far sooner than anyone had predicted. The now 17-year-old Joe admitted he was "reconciled to a long apprenticeship in the reserves", but Hibs had a problem. Reilly, so key in attack, had been struggling for some time with a knee injury. Manager Hugh Shaw handed Joe his first team debut in Hibs' opening competitive game of the 1957-58 season, a League Cup tie away to Airdrie on 14 August. The occasion proved less than memorable, with Hibs losing 4-1. Joe would have to wait six agonising weeks before he was given another chance, which would again come against Airdrie. By the time he made his league debut, on 28 September, Hibs had already been eliminated from the League Cup at the group stage. The league meeting proved more successful, with Hibs winning 4-0. Reilly, with one of his last goals for Hibs, was among the scorers, but Joe had again failed to find the net. After missing the league win over Falkirk, Joe was brought in to replace Reilly in a Monday night friendly against Hearts, in the first match under the new floodlights at Tynecastle. Inside forward Tom Preston, regarded by some Hibs fans as the "sixth member of the Famous Five", scored a hat-trick in the 4-2 victory, with Joe grabbing the other goal.

It was a watershed. Joe scored twice in the next match – a 2-0 league win over Queen's Park – his first goals at Easter Road, in a match that saw Reilly move to inside right to accommodate this explosive new talent. Hibs were next up against English opposition when Tottenham Hotspur, whose side included the likes of Danny Blanchflower and Bobby Smith, travelled to Easter Road for the latest instalment of the Anglo-Scottish Floodlit League.

With Reilly, still recovering from a cartilage operation, watching from the sidelines, Joe tore Spurs apart by scoring a hat-trick in a 5-2 win. The supporters who had, until recently, been chanting for Reilly, were now singing for the 17-year-old from Motherwell. "He is more than a new personality. He is a new Easter Road idol of the fans," announced journalist Bob Scott. "Not since Reilly has a Hibs player received such an ovation. And the curious thing is that Joe is a player in the Reilly mould. Same style, same aggressiveness, same powerful shot."

Joe followed up his sensational showing against Spurs with his first competitive hat-trick, this time in a 3-2 league win away to St Mirren. As far as his team-mates were concerned, it looked like a worthy successor to Reilly had been found. "Joe was rattling in the goals so he became a first-team regular very quickly," says former Hibs winger John Fraser. "He was like Lawrie in that, if he got clean through, one-on-one with the keeper, you would bet your life on him scoring. He didn't really blast the ball, he passed it into the net."

The brilliant Gordon Smith, meanwhile, was taken aback by his young team-mate's turn of pace. "One moment, he's facing his own goal – the next, he's whipped round like a top and streaking for goal," he said. "His pace is unbelievable at times and he's learning the business very fast."

But while Joe continued to score regularly, Hibs' league form began to falter. This included a miserable run of five straight defeats – three of them at home – during December and January. Rubbing salt in the wounds of the Easter Road faithful was the fact that their free-scoring Edinburgh rivals, Hearts, were on a seemingly unstoppable march towards their first league title since 1897. Although there was still hope of a decent finish in the league, only the Scottish Cup, a competition they hadn't won since 1902, could salvage Hibs' season. They had been drawn away to Dundee United and, after battling out a 0-0 draw at Tannadice, Joe scored in a 2-0 win in the replay at Easter Road to send Hibs through to the third round.

But in the eyes of Hibs supporters, and indeed the players, this was likely to be the end of the road. Standing between Hibs and a place in the quarter-finals were Hearts. Even with two of their celebrated "Terrible Trio" – Alfie Conn and Willie Bauld – struggling with injury, Hearts had already racked up a century of goals in the league. Under the inspirational captaincy of a young Dave MacKay, the prolific Jimmy Wardhaugh, together with Jimmy Murray and Alex Young, had formed another terrifying trio, one that had enjoyed results such as 9-0 against East Fife, 8-0 against Queen's Park and 9-1 against Falkirk. Tommy Walker's side, who had won the Scottish Cup two seasons previously, were steamrollering virtually everyone in their path. With Hearts unbeaten at home and seemingly scoring at will, few gave Hibs any chance of overcoming their intimidating opponents, particularly as they had already been beaten by Hearts both home and away in the league. And with the match on 1 March to be played at Tynecastle, the outlook appeared even more bleak.

"Hibs had been playing badly, Hearts had been playing well," said Joe, with typical understatement. "When we were drawn against them in round three, I don't think anyone gave us a chance. It was to be a walkover for Hearts. I don't believe even Hibs' most faithful supporters thought we were in the running."

If there was a single game that truly announced Joe's arrival as a Hibs superstar, however, this was it. Joe scored all four goals in a 4-3 win, progress in the Cup was secured and a legend was born. Alex Young, later revered by Everton fans as the "Golden Vision", enjoyed great success at Hearts but admits, on that day, the men in maroon were overshadowed. "Hearts were running away with the league and we were huge favourites to beat Hibs in the Cup," he says. "But Joe was terrific. He was diving in for headers, as brave as anything, and he was as quick as a greyhound. There weren't many players faster than Joe and it was obvious to anyone who saw that game at Tynecastle that he was a special player."

Although it's a day he would rather forget, former Hearts goalkeeper Gordon Marshall has clear memories of Joe's first goal, which cancelled out Johnny Hamilton's opener. Marshall, who was only a year older than Joe, says: "Willie Ormond kicked the ball against the bar, it bounced down and Joe was just standing there to get a wee tap-in. I thought, 'Oh, ye wee bugger ye!'"

Joe put Hibs ahead just before the half-hour mark, leaving Hearts centre-half Jimmy Milne for dead before firing past Marshall from 20 yards. "If you tried to play offside against Joe, he would sit with the last man and 'peow', he was off like a bullet," says Marshall. "Jimmy Milne was a good footballing centre-half but he had no pace at all and he couldn't handle Joe. He used to try to push us out but Joe had so much pace that he absolutely destroyed us that day."

Wardhaugh equalised just after half-time, but another two goals from Joe in the space of 15 minutes seemed to have all but ended Hearts' dreams of a league and Cup double. Murray pulled a goal back for Hearts in the 89th minute but, when the referee waved aside a late shout for a penalty, the strike was a mere consolation. Hibs goalkeeper Lawrie Leslie, who had made a series of good saves during the match, was carried off the pitch shoulder-high by delirious Hibs supporters, while Joe could reflect on the fact that his killer instinct had put his team in the last eight of the Scottish Cup. Not even a booking, for bending over and allowing the unfortunate Milne to fly over the top of him for a second time, could take the shine off his performance. "Everything seemed to go right from the first kick," he said later. "I'll never forget the excitement of it, on the field, and in the dressing-room afterwards."

Joe took his Scottish Cup tally for the season to seven in four matches when he scored twice in the 3-2 quarter-final victory over Third Lanark to set up a semi-final with Rangers. Watched by a combined total of more than 150,000 people, a 2-2 draw at Hampden on 5 April was replayed four days later, when Eddie Turnbull's penalty and John Fraser's winner put Hibs into their first Scottish Cup final for over a decade. Like their opponents, Clyde, they would be going for their third Cup win. The difference was that, while Hibs hadn't triumphed since 1902, Clyde had lifted the trophy as recently as 1955, after beating Celtic in a replay.

On 21 April, five days before the final, Joe made way for Lawrie Reilly to play at centre-forward in what would be his final appearance in a Hibs shirt. Made captain for the evening, poetically, Reilly got on the scoresheet in Hibs' 3-1 victory over Rangers. It was a fitting end to a wonderful career. In the words of former England captain Jimmy Armfield, "As Reilly bowed out, Hibs were lucky to have a top-class replacement in Joe Baker."

Reilly, interviewed for this book before his death in July 2013, admitted that Joe was a natural successor to his Easter Road crown. "I was a reasonable centre-forward," he said, modestly, "so it didn't bother me when Joe first emerged on the scene, but then I got my knee injury and Joe got his big chance. I had been playing for Hibs since I was 16 but I had to end my career at just 29. I'd like to have played on for a few more years but Joe was definitely a worthy replacement. Although I was mainly a centre-forward, I was quite versatile, in that I played both outside-right and outside-left for Hibs and Scotland. I got to play alongside Joe on only a few occasions for Hibs, playing at inside-right or out on the wing, but Joe was really just a pure centre-forward. I don't think he played any other position for Hibs. His pace was very enviable – he was like greased lightning. Eight out of ten of his goals were due to his pace."

Gerry Baker adds: "Lawrie was our hero. Even if we were only playing football in the park, we wanted to be Lawrie Reilly, but Joe was a better player. He had this calmness about him. He had very big boots to fill at Hibs but he just fitted in. He scored from the very beginning – he couldn't stop scoring."

On 26 April 1958, Joe Baker stepped out on to the Hampden Park pitch for the biggest moment of his young footballing life. As he soaked up the noise of more than 95,000 spectators at the national stadium, he could barely believe that, less than a year ago, he was playing Junior football with Armadale Thistle. Unlike their third-round match against Hearts, Hibs went into the final as favourites, with most neutrals hoping that, with Hearts having already wrapped up victory in the league, the men in green and white could complete an Edinburgh double.

A swirling wind meant conditions were far from ideal, but Hibs' troubles were only beginning. Andy Aitken, who had scored in the semi-final against Rangers and who had helped create so many goals for others during the season, was injured in a tackle after only 15 minutes and, in the days before substitutions, the winger was forced to struggle on. After 28 minutes, John Coyle, a frequent scorer for Clyde since his move from Dundee United, took aim from outside the box. It looked like his shot was going wide, but John Baxter, the unfortunate Hibs left half, stuck out a boot and the deflection diverted the ball past Lawrie Leslie.

Hibs thought they had rescued the game when Joe converted a cross by Aitken, who was still battling away bravely despite his injury. The referee was quick to spot Joe's use of the hand, however, and the equaliser wasn't given. In the end, the equaliser didn't come at all and Hibs left the field knowing that yet another chance for Scottish Cup glory had passed them by.

Deflated, disappointed and ultimately without silverware, Hibs' season petered out. The club finished a disappointing ninth in the league, with a goal difference of minus one. It was a different story in the west of the city, with champions Hearts scoring a British record-breaking 132 goals as they beat runners-up Rangers by 13 points. Nevertheless, with 22 competitive goals in his debut season, the arrival of Joe had at least given Hibs supporters something to cheer about.

With the scintillating 17-year-old leading the charge, there would surely be many more chances to win trophies in the seasons to come. But back in Motherwell, having thrown in the towel at Chelsea, the future of Gerry Baker looked considerably less bright.

5
Cooking with Motherwell

As 18-year-old Gerry Baker watched a steady stream of human faeces floating in his direction, he took a moment to reflect on what might have been. He thought that maybe living in London wasn't so bad after all. Perhaps there were, indeed, worse things in life than playing in the reserves for one of England's biggest football clubs, even if it wasn't in his preferred position. Having said that, he'd probably rather have been anywhere at that precise moment than painting pipes down a sewer, doing his best to keep down his breakfast amid a river of human shit.

Several weeks had passed since he took the decision to leave Chelsea, citing homesickness and a lack of first-team opportunities as his reasons for quitting. He had returned to the family home in Motherwell and settled back into work as an apprentice painter and decorator as he continued to weigh up his sporting options. The problem with being "the worst painter and decorator in history", however, was that jobs such as painting pipes and railings at sewage works became par for the course. "I was given all the shite jobs, literally in some cases," he says. "I couldn't eat for two or three days and the boys at work ate all my sandwiches because I couldn't face eating them. They thought it was hilarious."

Fortunately for Gerry, while he had been away in London, Motherwell had appointed a new manager; one who, like Ted Drake, had an eye for talented young players. Bobby Ancell, a former Scotland international, was assembling an attractive side that was beginning to take the Scottish First Division by storm. As well as experienced professionals such as Charlie Aitken and Alex "Baldy" Shaw, Motherwell were amassing a plethora of promising youngsters. They became known as "Ancell's Babes", and included a forward line of Billy Hunter, Sammy Reid, who played alongside Joe for Scotland Schoolboys, Pat Quinn, Andy Weir, and an 18-year-old centre-forward called Ian St John.

After returning from London, Gerry had been training with Motherwell in order to retain his fitness. Recognising his talent, his pace and the fact that there would be no possibility of him feeling homesick, Ancell signed Gerry for £750 on 14 December 1956. While grateful to be given the chance to be signed by a club only six weeks after walking out on Ted Drake and Chelsea, Gerry quickly discovered that breaking his way into a forward line described by future Liverpool legend St John as "five little wizard boys all in a row", wasn't going to be easy.

Gerry says: "I found it difficult to get into the team but, even when I did, I couldn't play where I wanted to play, which was at centre-forward. Because of my speed, I was playing outside left or outside right. Once St John broke into the team and couldn't stop scoring, I was experiencing exactly the same problem as when I was at Chelsea, only this time it was Saint rather than Greavsie that was scoring all the goals." God help us, Gerry must have thought, if those two ever formed a partnership.

Although St John, two months Gerry's junior, seized the No.9 shirt at Fir Park with both hands, Gerry made his first-team debut a few matches before the future television pundit.

On 8 April 1957, three days shy of his 19th birthday and with Motherwell fourth in the table, Ancell selected Gerry to play on the wing in a league match away to Dundee. The match ended in a 3-1 defeat – their fifth in succession. Gerry wasn't selected for the next two games, which saw Motherwell lose to Queen's Park and then Aberdeen, but he continued to gain valuable experience, helping Motherwell Reserves win the Scottish Second XI Cup by scoring the winner in the first-leg victory over Celtic. His second match for the first team came in a midweek match in Dumfries, on 24 April, where he followed up an assist for Pat Quinn with his first goal in professional football to give Motherwell a 2-1 lead over Queen of the South. The match finished 2-2, but it finally ended Motherwell's run of seven defeats in a row.

Gerry's first-team bow at Fir Park came the following season, in the League Cup against Aberdeen on 17 August. Although it was another defeat, *The Motherwell Times* gave a glowing appraisal of the lightning-quick teenager. There were, said the report, "cheers of delight that echoed round the stand when young Gerry Baker made his presence felt in the early minutes of the game". It added: "Baker's display was the outstanding feature of the game from Motherwell's point of view. He showed skill, quickness of reaction, strength in running and, particularly pleasing in a Motherwell winger, an ability to hit the ball on the run first time. His value to the team can't be emphasised too much."

That may have been the case, but Gerry didn't get another run out in the firsts until 26 October. Part of the problem, says Gerry, was his proneness to cramp. He adds: "During the summer, I took part in a lot of sprinting competitions, with Joe acting as my manager. We had a good hustle going on, but I don't think putting so much effort into two sports helped my career at Motherwell. I might have played more games for them if I hadn't been so stupid. The manager can't have found it helpful to have a player who kept seizing up. He knew I could play but he had his reservations. He told me, 'You've got the best legs but they keep giving in.' The cramp wasn't something I really got control over until after I left Fir Park."

The problem was summed up in a reserve match report, which said that: "Baker's main trouble is not so much concerned with controlling the ball but controlling himself". From a personal point of view, the league match at home to Falkirk signalled the brightest spell of Gerry's brief Motherwell career. It was another defeat, this time 5-2, but his goal to put his side 2-1 up, described by *The Herald* as "a spectacular shot after a thrilling run", was enough to put him in the side for the next home game against Raith Rovers. It was another loss, but he finally tasted victory in the next match, scoring the only goal of the game away to Kilmarnock.

After another three-match absence, he scored his side's fourth goal in a brilliant 4-1 win over Aberdeen and kept his place for the next three games. It was only the beginning of January, but Gerry had played his last competitive match of the 1957-58 season in the Motherwell first team. He did play in the Lanarkshire Cup semi-final against Hamilton, scoring a hat-trick in a 6-0 win, but he wanted regular football.

It was frustrating, Gerry admits, but playing in the comfort of his home town had its advantages. "It was great to get the chance to be at the same club as Charlie Aitken, who was my favourite player when I was a kid," he says. "Joe and I knew them all because we used to go to all of Motherwell's home games together." Among the Fir Park youngsters, too, there was a great sense of camaraderie.

"We were all boys together," says Gerry. "You could've thrown a blanket over Lanarkshire and all the players were there – from Motherwell, Hamilton and Wishaw, and I think there's a lot to be said for that when you're playing football."

He may have been granted a second chance at a football career after quitting Chelsea, but that wasn't going to stop Gerry having fun when he got the chance. "He was always having a laugh and didn't seem to take things too seriously," says Billy Hunter. "I remember when a number of us were staying in a hotel following a match up in Aberdeen. Our captain that day was Baldy Shaw, who was an old seasoned veteran. Bobby Ancell had told him to look after us young boys at the hotel. There were about seven or eight of us, including Gerry, Ian St John and Pat Quinn. We were desperate to go to the dancing and have a couple of beers, but Shaw said we had to stay in the hotel bar. He said, 'You're going to sit there all night with me and that's it.'"

Gerry, dressed in his latest sharp suit, was having none of it. "I wanted to go to the dancing, so I told the lads we could go out the fire escape outside my bedroom window," he says. "Stupidly, I climbed on to the balcony and the whole ladder opened up and fell to the ground with me hanging on to it for dear life. I got oil and dirt all over my shoes, but we still went to the dancing."

It was not the kind of behaviour, admits Hunter, that would ever endear Gerry to Bobby Ancell. At the beginning of the 1958-59 season, Ancell selected Gerry for one more match in the first team, a 5-2 League Cup defeat at home to Partick Thistle, before the manager's patience with his flying winger ran out. "Bobby was an old-fashioned manager and he wanted everything done by the book," explains Hunter. "He wasn't the flashiest dresser. He used to wear jackets with leather patches and looked a bit like a schoolteacher. We were all wearing the club blazers and flannels and Gerry came in one Saturday wearing the latest coat and scarf and shoes. Ancell said, 'If you don't change your apparel and smarten up you'll be out the door.' Gerry thought he was being funny, but Ancell was being deadly serious."

Ian St John had already been warned about his appearance and, with both eyes firmly on the career ladder, he trotted off immediately to get his hair cut and to buy "trousers that weren't too tight at the bottoms".

Perhaps inspired by the rebel-themed movies of the era, Gerry took a different tack. "I don't know why Ancell didn't like me," he says. "I wasn't going to be playing, as usual, and I was just standing in the dressing room, wearing a new £12 coat that my mother had bought me. That's when he had a go at me – my dress-style, my hair, it was one thing after another. I said to him, 'I've just left Motherwell train station and there's a newspaper seller down there who's better dressed than you are, so don't get on at me about my new coat.' So that was me out the door at Motherwell. It turned out to be the best thing that could've happened. I wasn't going to stand there and let him have a go at me. Besides, I had good hair."

It wasn't the first time Gerry's mouth had got him into trouble, and it wouldn't be the last. Sometimes his arguments with management would be articulate and reasoned but, with Ancell, the rebellious youth was simply in Marlon Brando-esque, don't-give-me-shit-about-my-new-threads mode. As he stood defiant in the dressing room, Gerry had only one question for Ancell: "Whadya got?"

The answer, which came almost immediately, was a transfer to St Mirren – a move that would change Gerry's life.

6
The Yank of Love Street

"Sometimes," says former St Mirren hero Jim Rodger, "it takes just one man to transform an entire team. At Love Street, that man was Gerry Baker." Unlike Motherwell, who had the goalscoring talents of Ian St John at their disposal, the "Buddies" of Paisley had problems finding a decent centre forward. One newspaper reported that the club had deployed 33 different players in the role since the early 1950s. Not even Gerry, with his positive outlook on life and unwavering belief in his own ability, could have imagined that, following his £2,000 move from Motherwell in November 1958, he would be able to fulfil this role quite so spectacularly.

From the moment he scored the winning goal against Hibs on his debut at Love Street on 22 November, getting the better of his younger brother in the process, everything seemed to fall into place for the 20-year-old. There was no Jimmy Greaves at St Mirren, no Ian St John and, at last, Gerry could enjoy centre stage. Having finished a lowly 13th in the league the previous season, Willie Reid's side were again struggling to give their supporters much to cheer about, least of all in the League Cup, where they had fallen at the first hurdle following a 6-1 thrashing at Clyde. "Gerry arrived at Love Street about a dozen games into the season," says Rodger. "We were struggling a bit near the bottom of the league and we weren't going many places."

Following his successful debut, Gerry scored another three league goals before the turn of the year, but it was only at the beginning of 1959 that he really found his shooting boots. Part of the reason was trainer Jimmy McGarvey's stretching routines, which helped Gerry overcome the cramp that had done much to hamper his career at Motherwell. And it would be St Mirren, not Motherwell, who would reap the rewards. Since their formation in 1877, St Mirren had won the Scottish Cup only once, in 1926. And, given their indifferent form in the league, there was nothing to suggest that their long wait would end any time soon – especially as they were due to kick off the 1958-59 competition on the evening of Friday 13 February. Saints had been given a bye to the second round, however, and the only unlucky party during the tie, the first ever floodlit match to be played at Love Street, turned out to be the hapless opposition – Peebles Rovers.

Gerry scored four and Tommy Bryceland three in a 10-0 demolition of the East of Scotland side. With each player on a bonus of ten shillings for every goal scored, the scoreline equated to an extra fiver each.

It may not have worked for Bobby Robson's England ahead of the 1988 European Championships against non-league Aylesbury, but sticking a hatful of goals past vastly inferior opponents seemed to do St Mirren's confidence the world of good. The following Saturday, Gerry scored in a 6-2 win at home to Dunfermline Athletic, but it was three days later, at Dundee's Dens Park, when the striker really started to get himself noticed. "Gerry's talent was typified in that match up at Dundee," says Rodger. "They were a very strong team at the time, and we beat them 6-4. Gerry scored four times. Ian Ure, who became Scotland's centre-half and who played alongside Joe Baker at Arsenal, was just starting out. Well, it was like a racehorse and a carthorse. I've never seen anyone quicker over ten yards than Gerry. He had this really distinctive running style, a circular motion – like a superfast tumbleweed. It was a strange style but it was incredibly effective and it helped him get so many goals.

"There were numerous occasions that I'd see him outstrip the opposition defence. Tommy Bryceland and Tommy Gemmell would play the killer passes and Gerry would race on to the ball and then glide it into the corner of the net. His finishing was remarkable. When he went through on the keeper, very seldom did he miss. Gerry Baker was not in the habit of ignoring chances."

Gerry certainly didn't want to ignore any chances when his previous employers, Motherwell, were the next league visitors to Love Street. The Steelmen – whose Babes were now in full flight – were enjoying a season of spectacular results on their way to an eventual third-place finish. This included an 8-1 thrashing of Third Lanark and a 6-1 win over Queen of the South. Gerry's pace and finishing wrought havoc with his former teammates, however, as he scored twice in a 4-1 win. "I always tried extra hard against Motherwell and their supporters hated me for that," he says.

The experience wasn't quite so enjoyable for Lizzie Baker, who was trying to divide her time equally between watching her sons in action. "My mother ended up being thrown out of the stadium," explains Gerry. "She was getting some soup when I scored and I ran behind the goal to celebrate in front of the Motherwell supporters, which I know I shouldn't have done, but it was difficult to resist. I think every single one of their fans wanted to strangle me. The woman giving my mother the soup said, 'Look at your big-headed son,' to which she replied, 'I've got two big-headed sons, so you can take your soup and stick it up your jumper' . . . or words to that effect.

The club printed an apology in *The Motherwell Times*, saying they wanted to say sorry to Mrs Baker for any inconvenience caused."

Gerry gave Motherwell fans even more to think about five days later, when he hit the goal that knocked them out of the Scottish Cup in a 3-2 win at Love Street. As expected, it was a hard-fought game, especially as Motherwell had swept aside First Division opponents Airdrieonians 7-2 in the previous round. Gerry clearly relished any chance to play against his former club. During his two years at Love Street, he served as a constant reminder to Motherwell fans that he was the one that got away. In the four games he played against his old side while at St Mirren, he scored six goals and enjoyed success on each occasion.

"When a club lets you go, then they've more or less ditched you, you're always going to bust a gut when you're playing against them," he says. "I had to prove to Motherwell that I should've been in *their* team."

Back in the league, March saw St Mirren suffer successive away defeats. It was hardly ideal preparation for their Cup quarter-final against Dunfermline Athletic but, for the third round in a row, they had been drawn at home, and Gerry kept his record of scoring in every round intact when he prodded home a late winner in a 2-1 victory. The reward was a semi-final clash with Celtic on 4 April. Historically, the odds didn't appear to be in St Mirren's favour. The Glasgow giants already had 17 Scottish Cup wins to their name and, even though they had failed to beat the Buddies in two attempts in the league, previous form was swaying fans' predictions.

"The thing to remember is that, when you're on a cup run, you think you can beat everybody," says former St Mirren winger Ally Miller. "But, when we were drawn against Celtic, we were more or less written off because of their reputation. However, they weren't a good side at the time and we were pretty good."

The result of the match, played at Hampden, suggests an even greater gulf between the two sides. Celtic simply couldn't cope with St Mirren's pace and movement. Miller scored twice and, blasting the ball past Frank Haffey from the edge of the area, Gerry put his side 3-0 up before half-time. His celebration, or rather the complete lack of it, strolling back to the centre circle, arms by his sides, demonstrated the kind of confidence that was now flowing through the St Mirren ranks. Bryceland made it 4-0 late on to seal a memorable victory and put St Mirren in their first Scottish Cup final since 1934.

On that occasion, they lost 5-0 to Rangers but, the way Willie Reid's side were performing in the competition, they would take to a much more level playing field against Davie Shaw's Aberdeen in the final on 25 April.

St Mirren won their final two games in the league to secure a seventh-place finish, but the only thing that really mattered was the upcoming date at Hampden Park. Shops in Paisley were decked out in black and white, local schoolchildren were singing "Baker is the best buy, the best buy, the best buy" to the tune of a famous McEwan's lager commercial, and 60,000 Saints supporters headed for Hampden. The match was watched by a total of 108,000 spectators and remains the last Scottish Cup final not involving either Rangers or Celtic to attract an attendance of more than 100,000.

"Can you imagine Aberdeen and St Mirren attracting that kind of crowd now?" asks Miller. "It was unbelievable." Not only would the match give St Mirren and Miller the chance to avenge their defeat to Aberdeen in the League Cup final of 1955, but, adds Miller: "We were on a £100 bonus to win."

Unlike the match four years previously, Aberdeen weren't the favourites. Struggling for First Division survival, they had shocked eventual champions Rangers 2-1 on the last day of the season at Ibrox. Fortunately for Rangers, second-placed Hearts had also lost. Aberdeen had also enjoyed a relatively easy route to the Cup final, not coming up against First Division opposition until they reached the last eight. But Aberdeen's slim hopes of causing an upset in the final were hampered when, after half an hour, right-back Dave Caldwell was injured and was forced out on to the wing. Ally Miller crossed for Tommy Bryceland to head St Mirren into the lead just before half-time before tapping home a second of his own on 65 minutes.

Becoming only the ninth player to score in every round of the Scottish Cup, Gerry got St Mirren's third with a beautiful chip over Aberdeen goalkeeper Dave Walker from the edge of the area with 14 minutes remaining. Aberdeen centre forward Hugh Baird fired in a consolation with virtually the last kick of the game. As St Mirren celebrated a 3-1 win, Davie McCrae, the club's record goalscorer and a hero of 1926, kept his promise of not opening his celebratory whisky until the trophy returned to Paisley.

Davie Lapsley, the captain who collected the Scottish Cup in 1959, took the first swig, but W.G. Gallagher, a reporter with the *Daily Record*, was in no doubt about which player had made the difference. "A few brief months previously anybody who had had the temerity to suggest St Mirren would triumph would have been looked upon as a candidate for a mental institution," he wrote. "That was before there had been transferred to the Paisley club from Motherwell a young centre forward named Gerry Baker. He cost a mere £2,000, but in less than half a season proved himself worth his weight in gold."

Manager Reid added: "Gerry has been more than a good player for us, he has been a mascot. Since he came to Love Street the St Mirren fortunes have taken a sharp turn for the better."

Although Gerry insists he and his younger brother were not competitive, the result at Hampden meant that, having succeeded where Joe and Hibs had failed the previous season and as the first Baker to win a senior trophy, he could claim the family bragging rights – at least for now. Gerry used to joke that their mother was "Mrs Hibs", but Lizzie insisted: "I don't support either Hibs or St Mirren – favouritism wouldn't be fair."

Joe's second season at Hibs had effectively come to an end at the beginning of February when he limped off with a ligament injury in a first round Cup replay win over Raith Rovers. "Joe had to sit with his leg up for two months, I don't know how he had the patience," says Gerry. "The Raith centre-half went right through him. I managed to get him back though, because I scored twice when we beat them a few weeks later."

Prior to his injury, Joe's second season at Hibs was proving even more successful than his first. He had scored 31 goals, including a run of 19 goals in 14 games. He also scored twice in Lawrie Reilly's testimonial match against an International Select. The injury put him out for two months, until the beginning of April. Not only did this mean that Joe missed the chance to get his own back on his brother for Hibs' defeat at Love Street (Gerry again scored the winner in a 1-0 victory at Easter Road), but he was also unable to help his club as they attempted to reach the Scottish Cup final for the second year running. They were beaten in the quarter-finals by Third Lanark.

Gerry, meanwhile, was able to savour his first piece of silverware and, today, the Cup-winning team of 1959 is fondly remembered by St Mirren supporters. "I'm still reminded about it regularly," says Rodger. "St Mirren won the Cup in 1926 and in 1987 but there seems to be something in the heart of the Saints fans that makes that team – our team – extra special. We're described as the 'Paisley Immortals', and I think that tells you everything."

At the beginning of the following season, 1959-60, barely a matchday went by without one or both of the Baker brothers' names appearing on the respective scoresheets of St Mirren and Hibs. By the time St Mirren travelled to Ibrox to play league champions Rangers on 17 October, Gerry was one of the most feared centre forwards in the country. Picking up where he left off after the Scottish Cup final, he had already scored 13 goals in as many matches. This included four goals in a 5-0 win away to Kilmarnock. The odds of him adding to his tally at the blue fortress in the west of Glasgow were slim, however, as St Mirren hadn't won a league match at Ibrox since 1904.

In the Rangers line-up were the fearsome full-backs Eric Caldow and Bobby Shearer. Known as "Captain Cutlass", Shearer was the epitome of a no-nonsense defender, and later earned notoriety for tackling a substitute who hadn't yet entered the field of play. Little wonder, then, that the man whose tackling former Rangers captain John Greig described as having "the force of a tank" took exception to the fleet-footed trickery of Gerry, who scored twice in an historic 3-1 victory. Greig said that one of Shearer's challenges on Gerry "sent him flying 10 yards into the Ibrox enclosure".

Thankfully, the tackle did no lasting damage and Gerry is able to laugh off the incident. "Shearer nearly killed me that day," he says. "I'd never heard Rangers fans booing their own players before. He went for me and he didn't miss." But far from acting as a catalyst to their league campaign, finally ending what Gerry called "the Ibrox hoodoo" seemed to have an adverse effect on St Mirren's results.

They embarked on a terrible run of five successive defeats, three of them at home. This included the match against Hibs on 7 November when Joe finally gained the upper hand on Gerry by scoring the winner in a 3-2 victory for the Edinburgh side. When the Scottish Cup kicked off again on 30 January, Saints had lost 10 out of the 15 league matches they had played since their win at Ibrox. It wasn't the best way to prepare for their defence of the trophy but, with the club languishing six points from the relegation zone, they were determined to give the Love Street supporters something to cheer about.

There was little doubt that, in being drawn at home to Glasgow University, St Mirren could hardly have asked for an easier tie. Nevertheless, in appalling winter conditions, the students and their colourful support, complete with Charity Day collection buckets, were hoping to make a game of it. Gerry Baker wasn't feeling particularly charitable. Ally Miller laughs at the memory of the game. "Gerry's probably told you 1,000 times about the time he scored 10 goals . . ."

Gerry is certainly proud of his achievement – scoring the biggest number of goals in a Scottish senior match in the twentieth century. The feat saw him outdo Ted Drake, his manager at Chelsea, and equal the single-game tally achieved by Luton Town's Joe Payne against Bristol Rovers in 1936. "The amazing thing is that, even though we won 15-0, it was still 0-0 after about 20 minutes," says Gerry. "I scored four headers before half-time, scored another six goals in the second half and then I left the pitch with 15 minutes to go. Their big goalkeeper kicked the ball right into my bollocks.

The ball was covered with ice and it was freezing. I felt like I'd been shot. The manager said, 'Come on son, keep going, there are only 15 minutes to go.' Sounding like a soprano, I said, 'I don't give a shit if there's 15 seconds to go. I'm going off!' Numb? I wish I had been."

Rodger remains sceptical. "I just don't think Gerry fancied spending any more time out in the snow," he says. "He was able to go into the nice warm dressing room and reminisce about his ten goals. Part of me could understand, because I spent the whole match getting pelted with snowballs by these blighters in the crowd as I was going down the wing. There wasn't a lot the referee could do about it. But Gerry could've set an all-time record if he'd stayed on the pitch. I think his attitude was, 'Well, I've done my bit – I'm off.' That was Gerry."

The result remains St Mirren's biggest-ever win, and Ally Miller is proud of his contribution on the day. "I scored the crucial 15th goal," he says. "Gerry and I scored 11 between us."

Glasgow University's Graduates Association magazine described the match as the highlight of the football season, noting that: "The score was high, but spectators of the match will remember that the University players did very well in atrocious conditions, and are to be congratulated on the sporting manner in which they played throughout the game."

Gerry's old pal Jimmy Greaves, on the other hand, took a slightly different view. "I'm told that when the University goalkeeper went to collect his degree he dropped it," he joked. Harsh, possibly, but nobody could deny the fact that the young players of Glasgow University had failed to provide St Mirren with a significant test.

The same couldn't be said of the next round. The Saints had been handed another home draw, but this time there were no students in the opposition ranks, only hardened professionals hell-bent on revenge for the 4-0 humiliation of last season's semi-final. One thing was for certain – Gerry wouldn't score ten goals against Celtic. The match was played on Saturday, 13 February 1960. The Hoops had won convincingly, 3-0, at Love Street in the league in December, but Rodger's goal secured a 1-1 draw to take the Cup tie to a replay at Celtic Park.

The replay, on Wednesday 24 February, turned out to be a thriller, with Gerry scoring St Mirren's second in a 4-4 draw. "It really was an incredible match," says Miller, who also scored for St Mirren. "Tommy Muirhead, a former Rangers player who had become a sports journalist, said that it was the best cup tie he had ever reported on."

But, before the advent of the penalty shoot-out, a second replay was required to decide who would go through to face Elgin City, the Highland

League outfit who, like everybody else, were waiting patiently on the outcome. In order to decide the venue of the next match, the referee tossed a coin. Celtic called correctly and the players were told to return to Parkhead the following Monday where, hopefully, a winner would finally be determined. Before then, St Mirren had to squeeze in a league fixture at Dundee's Dens Park, where they lost 3-1 and, says Miller, the punishing schedule was beginning to take its toll.

"What you have to remember is that St Mirren were a part-time club in those days, whereas Celtic were full-time," he says. "We had to change our side for the second replay. We brought in some players – older ones that could hardly run, I'm afraid, and we were outplayed in the end."

Miller does suggest, however, that there may have been an additional reason for the eventual 5-2 scoreline. "Jack Mowatt could be quite a controversial referee," he says. "He was in charge of the Real Madrid-Eintracht Frankfurt European Cup final at Hampden a few months later and he gave a penalty in that match that might or might not have been a foul. When we were losing 2-1, we went up the field and equalised. Mowatt blew for offside but the linesman didn't have his flag up. I went over and said, as you did in those days, 'Excuse me sir, the linesman's not got his flag up.' He turned to me and said, 'One more word out of you, Miller, and you'll be off. I remember thinking, 'He's determined to get this game finished!' He just wasn't having it. Not that Celtic weren't worthy winners, of course."

With the holders of the famous trophy finally eliminated from the competition, Gerry and the rest of the St Mirren squad needed to pick themselves up quickly. Ten league matches remained and the club's First Division survival was far from guaranteed. The resumption of league duties couldn't have got off to a worse start, with Stirling Albion dishing out a 7-0 drubbing at Love Street. What made the defeat worse was the fact that it was only Stirling's sixth victory of the campaign.

Fortunately, Gerry was on target in St Mirren's next two matches, 3-1 victories away to Hibs and Airdrie, but, with only two games remaining, they were still not mathematically safe. A 4-2 defeat at home to Partick Thistle did little to settle the nerves, but Dundee's win over Stirling was enough to ensure that the club who had humiliated St Mirren only a few weeks earlier would be the ones playing Second Division football next season.

First Division status preserved, the season ended on a positive personal note for Gerry, as he found the net against both halves of the Old Firm in the last two games – a 1-1 draw at home to Rangers and a 3-3 draw at Celtic. Thanks in no small part to his remarkable feat against Glasgow

University, Gerry was once again Saints' top scorer, with a total of 33 goals for the season.

"For a winger, I scored quite a few goals and Gerry always says he would've scored more if I wasn't getting so many myself," laughs Rodger, who scored in all three Cup games against Celtic. He used to shout, 'Cross it Jim! Cross it Jim! For God's sake cross it Jim . . . great goal Jim!' He had two tremendous inside-forwards in Tommy Bryceland and Tommy Gemmell, who were the masters of the accurate pass, but Gerry was a terrific striker and such a valuable asset to the team. What was obvious at the time with football was an attitude of, 'We'll score more than you,' whereas today it's more a case of 'We'll concede fewer than you.' With Gerry in the side, we were always likely to score. He was also an excellent chap to have in the team and in the dressing room. You never got him down. He was always bouncy and optimistic and really good company. He also wasn't given to talking about himself, his exploits or his capabilities. He was just happy to play football."

The question, though, was how long would Gerry be happy to play his football in Scotland? The lure of England was strong, as his younger brother knew only too well.

7
Lion Cub

If there was one thing Joe Baker had in abundance, aside from an unerring capacity to find the net, it was confidence. Perhaps nothing demonstrated this better than when, towards the end of his first season at Hibs, he told John Gibson of the *Edinburgh Evening News*: "I'd just love to play for England."

Never before had Gibson heard a young man with a Scottish accent voice such a desire, let alone a former Scotland Schoolboy international. If he had, he'd have taken him for a madman or a fool. But Joe Baker was neither. He was simply a young footballer with an insatiable appetite for success and, as the international laws of the time had decreed that the ultimate level could only be reached in a white shirt, then so be it. Joe also told John McPhail, the former Celtic and Scotland player turned *Daily Record* sports reporter, that playing for England was one of two footballing ambitions – the other being to score a winning goal for Hibs in the Scottish Cup final.

His debut season – 1957-58 – had seen him almost achieve the latter aim at the first time of asking. As for the former, it was the England captain, Billy Wright, who helped bring Joe's nationality to the attention of the English media. Following Hibs' Floodlit Cup match against Wolves in October 1957, in what was only Joe's seventh game for Hibs, Wright said: "He's a terrific proposition . . . and he's English."

Joe's first steps towards international football with England came immediately after his four-goal heroics against Hearts in the Scottish Cup in March 1958. It came in the form of a letter from Sir Stanley Rous, secretary of the Football Association, to Hibs chairman Harry Swan, asking for permission to play the 17-year-old in England's Youth and Under-23 teams. "We will give England every co-operation," said Hibs manager Hugh Shaw. "We feel it is an honour for our club by their asking for Joe Baker."

When England's Under-23s played Wales in Wrexham the following month, it was Middlesbrough's Brian Clough who wore the No.9 shirt. But their next game wouldn't be until September, against Poland, by which time Clough would be over the age limit. Yet despite the official approach by the Football Association, there were still doubts that England would break with 90 years of tradition by picking a Scotland-based player.

When asked to clarify the situation regarding Joe, Walter Winterbottom, manager of the Senior and Under-23 sides, said: "England has never had anything against Englishmen playing outside the country. The reason for a wrong slant being put on the situation is that – and this applies to Wales as well as Scotland – there have been so few Englishmen in that position. Any Englishman, no matter where he is playing, will *always* be considered for the England team. We are always looking for natural talent, and are always ready to use it."

Joe continued to put his natural talent to good use at the start of the 1958-59 season, when he scored a hat-trick in a 4-2 victory over Aberdeen in the League Cup. By this stage, Arsenal were one of a number of clubs reportedly making enquiries about the now 18-year-old's availability. Harry Swan's response was emphatic, if mildly over the top. "As far as I am concerned, I would rather burn down our grandstand than see him sold," he said.

Nevertheless, he was more than happy for England to assess his star youngster's ability. On 13 September 1958, in a league match at second-place Motherwell, Joe was told that two England Under-23 selectors, Sam Bolton and Syd Collings, would be taking in his performance at Fir Park. Typically unfazed, Joe scored twice and set up the other three as Hibs won 5-2, a stunning performance that led Bolton to proclaim: "He is just about the best centre forward proposition I've seen this season."

Bolton's comment prompted a "'Scot' to lead England?" headline in the *Daily Mirror*.

But while blown away by Joe's skill, former Celtic, Manchester United and Scotland forward Jimmy Delaney was still not convinced that the England selectors would make such a bold choice. "He's the best centre I've seen for years," said Delaney. "He's excellent with both feet, and his acceleration is terrific. Pity he cannot play for Scotland. It doesn't worry me. I don't think English selectors would pick a player from Scotland when they have so many in England."

For once, Delaney was wide of the mark. "A few nights later, when I reported at Easter Road for training, I was told that I had been picked for the England Under-23 side against Poland at Sheffield," recalled Joe. "There couldn't have been a happier young man in Scotland that night."

An official letter of confirmation from the FA arrived the following day, further reinforcing the opinion that, as Glasgow sports journalist James Sanderson put it so wonderfully, Joe was "not a teenage comet doomed to flash across the football firmament and then fade away in a trail of might-have-been sparks".

Hibs excused Joe from a Monday night friendly against Bayern Munich to allow him to travel to Hillsborough and meet up with his new English team-mates. "Walter Winterbottom made me feel at home right away," said Joe. "There were some wisecracks from some of the players about my Scottish accent, but it was all in good fun."

At 18 years and 69 days, Joe was the youngest member of the England team selected to face Poland, in what would be the first ever meeting between the two nations. The England line-up contained a number of familiar names, including Jimmy Greaves, Jimmy Armfield, the captain, as well as Albert Scanlon and Bobby Charlton, both of whom had survived the Munich Air Disaster seven months earlier. Two days before the match, the England Under-23s beat Sheffield United 3-1 in a warm-up game at Bramall Lane. Joe teed up one of Greaves's two goals, while Charlton, already a senior England player, scored the other. "I was satisfied with this very young side," said Winterbottom afterwards. "I thought Baker fitted in very well."

Joe's two inside-forwards, Charlton and Greaves, also shared the goals against Poland two days later, with Charlton scoring a hat-trick in a 4-0 win. Although Joe failed to get himself a goal in front of a crowd of more than 38,000, he crossed the ball for Greaves to open the scoring and said: "I have learned a great deal. It was a wonderful experience playing in the same team as Bobby Charlton."

Winterbottom was impressed with Joe's commitment, saying: "The boy had a grand, and most unlucky debut. Time and again he was just inches from scoring with the chances which cropped up. He is very good with his head, and he gave 90 minutes of full-out endeavour. We were pleased with him." Charlton was equally impressed: "Young Joe was most unfortunate," said the Manchester United youngster. "He tried so hard and played very well." Polish centre-half Stanislaw Oslizlo, who would go on to win 57 caps for his country at senior level, added: "Baker was a most elusive opponent. He is a very good and a very clean player. He will go far."

It was Winterbottom himself who had come up with the idea of the England Under-23s, who played their first match in 1954. He said: "The formation of an England Under-23 team is proof we are entering a new era of long-term England team-building with our finest young talent. The Under-23 team is not an England 'B' team, nor is it England reserves. Should all proceed to plan, it will be the future of English football at international level."

Stoke City left-back Tony Allen who, like Joe, was making his England debut against Poland, says: "The standard of the England Under-23 side was really high. That's obvious when you see the number of players in that line-up, including myself and Joe, who went on to become full internationals. It was more of an obvious stepping stone, not like today, where a lot of the England Under-21 players don't get near the senior side. With the Under-23s you would get players, such as Bobby Charlton, who would play for the senior side as well. We played in front of nearly 40,000 at Hillsborough, which shows how good a side we were. Joe was a great centre forward. Throughout his career, if he got ten chances, eight of them would end up in the back of the net."

Not, unfortunately for Joe, on his debut for the Under-23s, although he denied his lack of goals had anything to do with poor service from his team-mates. "I couldn't help noticing that the Scottish papers were saying that the other English forwards weren't giving me passes or chances," he said later. "I must admit that no such ideas ever entered my head."

Joe rediscovered his shooting boots at domestic level, scoring three goals in his next three league matches for Hibs, before he was selected to play against Czechoslovakia at Norwich City's Carrow Road three weeks later.

Again, however, it wasn't to be Joe's night. Playing in what would eventually become famous red shirts, Charlton and Greaves, the rising superstars playing on either side of the Hibs teenager, were the ones who grabbed the glory. Charlton had actually played for the full England side in between the two Under-23 matches, scoring twice in a 3-3 draw against Northern Ireland. Meanwhile, Joe didn't do himself any favours with selectors against the Young Czechs, passing up several chances, one of which saw him slipping and missing his kick with only the goalkeeper to beat. He did square the ball to Greaves to put England 2-0 up before half-time, which at least meant Joe could return to Scotland knowing that he made a telling contribution to his international cause.

The Under-23s didn't have another game until March, but Joe's league form for Hibs, including hat-tricks against Third Lanark, Celtic and Queen of the South, meant he was strongly favoured to retain his place. However, the same injury that robbed Joe of a chance to help Hibs reach a second successive Scottish Cup final also denied him a third England cap, with Jimmy Murray of Wolves being given the nod against France.

In a season that saw Hearts finish runners-up to Rangers, Hibs finished 10th, three places behind Gerry's St Mirren. But despite sitting out two months of the season through injury, Joe finished top scorer in Scotland with 25 league goals and 30 in all competitions.

It was no surprise, then, that interest in Hibs' teenage sensation was high. As well as Arsenal, Liverpool, Newcastle and Wolves were all rumoured to be making enquiries.

Telling all of Joe's suitors, in no uncertain terms, that their star striker was not for sale, Hibs set off on a post-season tour to Spain, with Barcelona their first port of call.

The fact that Hibs were outplayed in a 5-1 defeat didn't stop the Catalan club, whose representatives, in the words of Hugh Shaw, "chased us all over Spain", making a £35,000 offer for Joe's services, a fee that would have broken the record for a Scottish-based player. But, like the English hopefuls, Barca were given short shrift by the Hibs hierarchy. The message was loud and clear: Joe Baker was not for sale – at any price.

Hibs' tour of Spain coincided with the England Under-23s' visits to Italy and West Germany, with Burnley's Ray Pointer scoring twice on his debut in a 3-0 win in front of 75,000 supporters in Milan.

The Under-23s' first match of the new 1959-60 season would be against Hungary at Goodison Park on 23 September. But even though he had already scored eight goals in what would become a record-breaking season at club level, Joe was not selected, with Pointer earning his second cap at centre forward. England had every reason to be nervous. This was the first time they had played the Magyars at Under-23 level, with the memories of their senior counterparts' 6-3 and 7-1 drubbings of 1953 and 1954 still fresh in the nation's collective memory. In comparison, a 1-0 defeat was far from a disaster, but a hat-trick for Joe in the 7-4 thrashing of Dunfermline followed by two goals in a 5-2 friendly win over Bolton reminded England what they were missing and gave Joe the chance to get back into the international fold.

He was selected to play for a Football Association XI against the British Army in Newcastle on Wednesday 22 October. The *Edinburgh Evening News* took great delight in the fact that Joe would be travelling to St James' Park with a rival from across the city – Gordon Marshall.

The Hearts goalkeeper, who Joe had tormented in the Scottish Cup two seasons earlier, was born in Farnham, Surrey, at the beginning of the Second World War. Like Joe, he spoke with a broad Scottish accent, but England's abundance of top-class goalkeepers had severely hampered his chances of an international call-up.

On 20 October, the club rivals were photographed by the local newspaper at Edinburgh's Waverley Station, buying their train tickets and setting off to stake their claim for a place in the upcoming Under-23 match against France. With National Service still in place, the Army side was a strong one. It included a forward line consisting of four Scots: Davie Wilson (Rangers), John White (Spurs), Alex Young (Hearts) and George Mulhall (Aberdeen); as well as Peter Dobing of Blackburn, who had recently earned his first cap for the England Under-23s against West Germany. While Marshall found himself lining up against a familiar figure in Tynecastle team-mate Alex Young, Joe was up against Hibs centre-half Jackie Plenderleith.

Joe was in electrifying form. After seeing two headers saved by Aldershot's Scottish goalkeeper Chic Brodie, he managed to bury a third to register his first goal in England colours. Marshall, too, did his international cause no harm when he saved a Wilson penalty in a 3-1 win for the FA XI.

The Under-23s' next match was against France at Sunderland's Roker Park on 11 November. The England selectors were due to announce the side a week beforehand and Joe's hopes must have been lifted by Winter-bottom's simple post-match comment: "I like Joe Baker."

The England manager had even more cause to like Joe two days later, when he scored a hat-trick in Hibs' 11-1 demolition of Ayr United. Joe was also aided in part by the fact that, at the request of the French, no player who had appeared at full international level would take part in the match. This meant there would be no place in the side for Greaves or Charlton, who between them had scored all seven of Young England's goals in Joe's two caps to date. Joe was duly selected to face France, while Marshall was named as reserve goalkeeper behind Tony Macedo – a player with some-thing of a national identity crisis of his own. Nicknamed "The Rock of Gibraltar", the Fulham star's place of birth was to prove a contentious issue that would ultimately prevent him ever winning a full England cap.

Despite something of a Scouser-first, Englishman-second mentality among Liverpool's inhabitants, there was no disputing the fact that Joe's birthplace entitled him to play for the country he left as a baby. But never in almost 90 years of competition had a footballer plying his trade in Scot-land been selected to represent England at the top level. On 18 November, Walter Winterbottom's senior players would be taking on Northern Ireland in the British Championships at Wembley Stadium – the home of English football. Would the selectors dare pick a Scotsman? Joe Baker's insatiable appetite for goals could well make the decision for them.

8
London Calling

In the late 1950s, Brian Howard Clough was one of the deadliest finishers in English football. Middlesbrough fans knew it, England fans knew it, and Clough himself certainly knew it. By the start of the 1959-60 domestic campaign, the outspoken striker had hit 40-plus goals in three consecutive seasons. He had terrorised defences throughout the English Second Division, winning legions of admirers, as well as ruffling a few feathers.

But for all his goalscoring prowess, only the England selection committee could ultimately decide whether Clough could do the same at international level. On 28 October 1959, with Clough now the grand old age of 24 and having just hit all five goals in a 5-0 win over an Irish League XI, the committee – with Walter Winterbottom as team manager – finally gave Clough his big chance. Disappointingly for England and Clough, however, the Home Championship match at Ninian Park ended in a 1-1 draw, with 19-year-old inside-right Jimmy Greaves scoring England's goal.

Eleven days later came what should have been the pinnacle of Clough's playing career, as he ran out on to the Wembley turf for a friendly against Sweden. This time England lost 3-2. It was a result met with jeers from the home support and, after only two appearances – one draw, one defeat and, perhaps crucially, no goals – Clough was dropped. He wasn't the only England player to be axed after the Sweden match, with Greaves and Bobby Charlton also among the casualties. But while great things were to come from those players, Old Big 'Ead's brief international career was over.

Clough arguably had every right to feel aggrieved, particularly when, in later life, he looked on in disbelief as England caps were dished out freely to far less gifted forwards. For all his achievements as a player, and his remarkable success as a manager, Clough's lack of international recognition remained one of his biggest bugbears. By 1980, he had won as many European Cups as he had England caps. Although, back in October 1959, Clough had no idea that he had played his last game for England, he knew that he had failed to impress at Wembley. Clough's mood didn't improve when, three days after the defeat to Sweden, Middlesbrough lost 5-0 to Leyton Orient. What made things worse was the fact that, even prior to the

England match, the young skipper's relationship with his Boro team-mates had completely broken down.

"Cloughie was the kingpin, he was the captain, and we were more or less made to jump for him," explains former Middlesbrough and England striker Alan Peacock. "He had been having a go at the lads in the local newspapers and it didn't go down well in the dressing-room. I wasn't a full-time pro at the time because I was in the Army. I only met up with the team on match days so I wasn't involved in the disagreement, but the others had more or less sent Cloughie to Coventry [the players had actually written to the board, demanding that he be stripped of the Middlesbrough captaincy]. After England lost to Sweden, he was in turmoil. I don't think he'd had a particularly good game."

With Clough angry with himself and Middlesbrough angry with Clough, the players headed north for a Monday-night friendly at Easter Road. Cleveland's finest was accustomed to coming up against Scottish players, but not one who was vying for his England place. The Scottish domestic season was only ten games old, yet Joe Baker had already found the net 16 times for Hibs. The most talked-about teenager in the country, who had given up his job as an apprentice welder to go full-time at Easter Road, had also scored four goals in the Scottish League Cup. "Joe was getting a lot of publicity at the time," says Peacock. "We were seeing a lot of the reports from Scotland so we knew how good he was."

Clough was undaunted by the young pretender, however, scoring one goal and setting up five in a 6-6 draw. Peacock, who scored twice that evening, recalls: "I squared the ball to Cloughie for his goal but all the lads rushed over to congratulate me rather than him." Despite Clough's contribution to the Middlesbrough cause, he was still eclipsed by Joe, whose team-mates were more than happy to offer their congratulations, not only on his hat-trick, but for setting up goals for Bobby Johnstone and Willie Ormond.

The report of the match in *The Daily Mirror* was far from complimentary to Clough, opining that his "leisurely style contrasted poorly with Baker's tremendous speed, crisp distribution and accurate shooting". It also suggested that Joe had been buoyed by the announcement, just hours earlier, that he had been selected to represent England's Under-23s for the first time in over a year.

After scoring the winner against Gerry's St Mirren that Saturday, Joe travelled to Newcastle at the beginning of the following week to meet up with his England team-mates ahead of a practice match at St James' Park. If the prospect of appearing for the England Under-23s against France was an exciting one, nothing could have prepared him for the news he was about to receive from Ron Greenwood. The coach revealed that, in just over a week's time, Joe Baker, a young man who had spent all but six weeks of his life in Scotland, would lead the England attack against Northern Ireland in a full international at Wembley.

"It was a big surprise because I didn't expect my cap," he told the press. "I feel very proud." He wasn't alone. Back home in Motherwell, Lizzie Baker said: "This is wonderful. I was always afraid that because Joe was born in Liverpool and played in Scotland, he would miss an English cap."

Knowing that he would soon be leading the line "for real", Joe had a superb match against France, thrilling the 26,500 fans at Roker Park by powering home a header shortly after half-time in a 2-0 win.

In a curious quirk, England's lead was doubled 15 minutes later by Chris Crowe of Leeds United. Like Joe, the Newcastle-born forward spoke with a Scottish accent. Raised in the Portobello district of Edinburgh, Crowe trained with Hearts as a youngster and, like his new international team-mate, appeared for Scotland Schoolboys against England. He won his only senior cap for England against France while playing for Wolves in 1962.

With Gordon Marshall also in the squad against the French Under-23s, the match at Roker Park featured what must surely go down as the most Scottish-sounding England line-up ever assembled. If Joe had any nervous energy about his upcoming England debut, he had plenty of outlets for it. He played in Hibs' return friendly against Middlesbrough at Ayresome Park the following evening, opening the scoring in a 4-3 victory (Clough got two this time round). On the Saturday he scored in Hibs' 4-2 defeat at Raith Rovers, before travelling down to London on the Monday to meet up with the England team. It was more history in the making. Joe's selection for the Under-23s against Poland a year earlier had been big news, but a call-up to the senior squad was something else entirely. Soon enough, football fans on both sides of the Border would know exactly who Joe Baker was and what he could bring to English football.

Never before had a footballer playing outside the English Football League been selected to represent the full national side. The distinction was unique until Bayern Munich's Owen Hargreaves made his England debut against the Netherlands more than 40 years later.

Joe said: "I had visions of being called a traitor. Not a bit. Hugh Shaw told me, 'You have broken the barrier, and as Scots we are proud of you. Your selection has proved that Scottish football is not second-rate. Go down and show them just how we can play up here.' So, even when pulling the England jersey over my head, I still felt, to some extent, I was really playing for Scotland. Not being big-headed, if I flopped for England the whole of Scottish football would be classed as rubbish."

Losing his place in the England side was difficult enough for Brian Clough, but it is tempting to think that losing it to a 19-year-old Scotsman gave a new definition to ignominy.

"I don't think he'd have thought about it in those terms," laughs Alan Peacock. "He'd have hated to lose his bloody England place to anybody – no matter who they were. Joe and Cloughie were entirely different players. Joe was very sharp, very quick, and he moved about well. Cloughie was a finisher – just a finisher. That's all he wanted to do. I remember Jimmy Greaves and Bobby Charlton telling me, when I went into the England team, that they could never actually play to Brian. The way we played at Middlesbrough, everything went through to Cloughie but, when he was with the England side, it was an entirely different set-up that didn't suit him. He played a certain way and I don't think England wanted to change their system for his benefit. Walter Winterbottom wanted a centre forward like Joe, who would move and run about, whereas Cloughie would say, 'This is where I score my goals so this is where I want you to put the ball.' When you look at his record though, he probably should've got more caps than he did."

Joe, on the other hand, had become impossible for the England selectors to ignore, and even an ego such as Clough's had to concede that the teenager from Lanarkshire was worthy of his chance. At 19 years and 123 days on the day of the match against Northern Ireland, Joe would be the third youngest England international since the War. Only Duncan Edwards, whose death following the Munich Air Disaster the previous February was still keenly felt by the nation's football fans, and Jimmy Greaves, who was 19 years and 86 days when he played against Peru in May 1959, were younger.

Like Clough, Joe was fortunate that England were willing to experiment with new players. Two of British football's most prolific strikers were among nine new faces England had called up in the space of three matches.

Joe earned his first cap alongside fellow debutants Ron Springett (Sheffield Wednesday), Ray Parry (Bolton) and West Ham's Ken Brown. Joe had actually played against Parry the previous month, when the Hibs striker scored twice in a 5-2 friendly win over Bolton at Easter Road. But even though it was surprising that three of England's brightest young stars, in Greaves, Charlton and Clough, had been dropped, it was the selection of Joe that raised the most eyebrows. With only two wins in eight matches since the start of the year, Winterbottom's side were struggling and, rather than delve once again into the English Second Division for a centre forward, the selectors had instead turned their attention to the land of their fiercest rivals.

The Glasgow newspaper, *The Bulletin*, claimed Joe's inclusion meant the selection committee had "made a striking condemnation of English football" and that "they have, in fact, said that there is no top-class English centre forward in the Football League at the present time".

And while everybody accepted that Joe's place of birth could not be helped, his nationality was still a source of some debate. "He was more Scottish than I was for God's sake!" joked Lawrie Reilly who, during a prolific Scotland career, scored against England on six occasions. "Billy Wright [105 appearances for England, most as captain] probably gave Walter Winterbottom the tip after we played Wolves in the Floodlight Cup and saw how good Joe was. I think he got a lot of teasing – we were all Scots of course. We tried to speak with English accents to annoy him, but he was a Scot through and through. For the FA to come up to Scotland to pick a player to play for England – it was completely unheard of. It was unique."

After his playing career was over, Joe admitted to having mixed feelings over his selection for England, saying, "Six weeks in Liverpool could never make me English. I was nothing else but Scottish. People always asked me why I didn't pick Scotland, but the rules did not change until it was too late." However, at the time he wrote: "It's hard to describe the thrill of pulling an international jersey over your shoulders. I experienced it as a schoolboy with a Scottish jersey, but I never dreamt I would be wearing the white jersey of England within another few years. I've been chaffed about being chosen for England, and been asked if I wouldn't rather have played for Scotland. The answer, of course, is no. Any player should be, and undoubtedly is, proud to be chosen for his country, for all the years I've spent in Scotland I still happen to be English by birth. When you think of the much wider field of choice they have over the Border, it's a terrific honour to be chosen for their international side."

Regardless of how he really felt about the situation, Joe's thick Scottish accent almost led to him missing his England debut. In a story that would become a favourite among fans in the Easter Road hospitality lounge long after his playing days were over, Joe recalled getting into a taxi at London Airport (now Heathrow) and telling the driver, with plenty of rolled 'R's, that he wanted to be driven to the Hendon Hotel. "That's where the England team are staying," replied the Cockney cabbie, before surreptitiously radioing for the police to take custody of the mad Scotsman in the back of his taxi. Fortunately, Joe was able to convince the boys in blue that he was, indeed, the Scotsman who had been sent for to try to revive England's fortunes.

Wolves stalwart Ron Flowers, who appeared in 40 consecutive England matches between 1958 and 1963, admits that hearing Joe's accent in the home dressing-room at Wembley was something of a novelty. "It was very strange having a real Scotchman playing for England," he says. "But Joe was a really nice fellah and a bit of a comedian. He had a Scottish accent in the England camp, so I suppose he had to have a good sense of humour. Things were certainly never dull when he was around. There was a big rivalry between England and Scotland, particularly during the era of the Home Championship, so one or two players didn't exactly make fun of Joe, but they referred to his accent quite a bit. Joe took it in good part. It wasn't malicious, but we did have a little dig at him as though he was a foreigner, calling him 'Scotty' and things like that."

Flowers is quick to point out, however, that nobody in the England side felt Joe was unworthy of his place. "It wasn't really a surprise that he got picked because he was a prominent player with his club and, at that time, I don't think the gap between English football and Scottish football was as great as it is today," he says. "Joe was always there or thereabouts in terms of selection and at the time he was first choice for England. He was what I used to call a typical Scots player. He was a fizzer. He was a bit nippy. He never really stood still. He was on the go all the time. Even when he wasn't in possession of the ball, he was always on the move."

While Flowers was able to accept the young Scot into the England fold, Sammy Reid, who played alongside Joe against England Schoolboys at Goodison Park four years earlier, says the sight of his former team-mate in a white shirt took some getting used to. "We lived about a mile apart in Wishaw," explains Reid. "He was a typical Scottish schoolboy – he hated England as much as the rest of us! But, in all seriousness, he was such a great player that he deserved to play with any international team . . . it was just unfortunate for the people of Scotland that he wasn't born up here. But, to be honest, when he got the call-up for England, everybody round here was chuffed about it."

None more so than Gerry, who made the trip down to London to watch the mid-week match, but only after helping his little brother get the required time off work. "Joe was working at Pickering's – a steelworks in Motherwell – as an apprentice welder," he explains. "He went to his gaffer and said: 'I'll have to have Wednesday to Friday off because I'm playing for England at Wembley.' You can imagine the look on his boss's face. I don't think he'd read the newspapers or he would've known all about it. I went to

Joe's work with him to explain the situation. I said to his boss, 'My brother is going to be making history.' His boss eventually agreed to let him have the time off so that he could play for England, on the condition that Joe came in on the Saturday morning to count all the steel ingots."

This monotonous task may have been designed to keep the striker's feet on the ground, but it hardly seemed necessary. Like everything else in life, Joe took becoming an international footballer in his stride, although things may have been different had he heard for himself the gripes of some supporters. "I'd gone down to watch Joe's debut. It was magic but I was getting an earache," says Gerry. "A fan sitting behind me kept moaning, 'Why did they pick a bloody Scotsman for England? Why didn't they pick Brian Clough?' I was doing my best to keep my mouth shut but, when Joe fired England into the lead after about 20 minutes, I turned round and said: 'That's why they picked a fucking Scotsman for England!' I couldn't take it any longer – what a shot it was, though. It went into the net like a bullet." And Joe wasn't finished there. After Billy Bingham had equalised with three minutes to go, the younger Baker brother jinked into the Northern Ireland box and squared for Ray Parry to score the winner in the dying seconds.

The Scotsman in the England jersey had made a point, winning over the doubters. Beneath the headline, "Baker is England's answer", Roy Peskett of the *Daily Mail* wrote: "At last! At last! At last! England have found a bold, bustling centre forward . . . Joe Baker, the centre forward England has been waiting for since Tommy Lawton, had given a wonder display."

The *Daily Express*, meanwhile, went with the headline: "Bravo McBaker – Darling of Wembley hope for England", under which Desmond Hackett gushed: "Thank Wembley for not so little Scots. I reckon Baker will be England's centre forward for as long as Scotland care to put him out on loan." Joe himself hadn't stuck around, boarding a plane back to Scotland just an hour after the final whistle.

"I was known as 'the ghost' to the journalists down there," he said. "I cracked one in from 25 yards on my debut at Wembley and they all wanted to talk to me. But I'd jumped out of the bath into a taxi and was home in Motherwell with my feet up before midnight."

With England not due to play again until April, Joe could get back to domestic duties with Hibs. That weekend, he scored twice in a 4-2 win over Dundee at Easter Road. He followed this up with a brace against Stirling Albion and a hat-trick, his third of the season, against Arbroath. In Hibs' 5-1 win over Ayr United on 12 December, Joe scored his 27th goal in 15 consecutive matches (including the two friendlies against Middlesbrough) in the space of two months. By the end of the campaign, he would smash the Hibs record for most goals in a season. Before that, though, he had the small matter of a second game for England to look forward to. This time it was an away fixture but, of all the England players, Joe would have the shortest journey to make. The other good news was that, this time, the local taxi drivers would have no difficulty understanding his accent.

9
Back Home

When Joe Baker was selected to appear for the England Under-23s against Scotland for a midweek clash on 2 March 1960, it seemed to many observers that the prophetic words of one journalist were about to come true.

Speculating, during Joe's second season at Hibs, that the "young prince of Scottish centre-forwards" wouldn't have long to wait before he was picked to play for England, Bob Hannah wrote: "King Joe the first of Scotland and England . . . no Nationalist outcries or international rows over this monarch. Only time I foresee an assassination plot being cooked up for this Baker is after he has doused the soccer hopes of the Scots in some future clash with the auld enemy on the Hampden turf, as he undoubtedly seems destined to do."

Destiny took a step closer when the latest England Under-23 line-up was announced, albeit one that would compete against the old enemy on the turf of Ibrox rather than Hampden. By this stage, Joe's inclusion was no longer a surprise. Since the start of the new decade, the centre forward had continued to be in the form of his young life, securing a point against Rangers at Ibrox and registering his fifth and sixth hat-tricks of the season against Third Lanark and then Clyde. And given his successful debut in an England shirt against Northern Ireland, Joe was a shoo-in to lead the young line in Glasgow. There was just one problem: for the first time in the striker's burgeoning international career, Hibs and England couldn't reach an agreement.

Hibs' second round Scottish Cup tie against Dundee, which had already been postponed seven times due to bad weather, was finally due to go ahead on 29 February – two days before the Under-23 match and the very day that Walter Winterbottom wanted Joe to report to Elland Road for a practice game against Leeds United. Naturally keen to play his strongest side, Hugh Shaw, the Hibs manager, informed Winterbottom that Joe would be required to play against Dundee, not Leeds. It was a decision that immediately cost Joe his fourth Under-23 cap, with Winterbottom moving Bobby Charlton into the centre and drafting in Jimmy Greaves to play at inside-left.

While it was bad news for Joe, Gordon Marshall was celebrating his first Under-23 cap, having been selected to play ahead of Fulham's Tony

Macedo. Like Joe, Marshall's availability was initially in doubt, but Hearts were able to play their postponed Cup tie with Kilmarnock the previous week.

Joe's disappointment, at least on the international front, didn't last long, with mid-table Hibs prepared to release him for the Under-23 match against the Netherlands two weeks later. Three days before the game at Hillsborough, Hibs' Scottish Cup campaign – the one that had cost Joe the chance to appear against Scotland – was ended by Rangers at Ibrox. Joe took the defeat out on the Dutch, scoring twice in a 5-2 win and getting the better of future *Escape to Victory* star Co Prins in the process.

More significantly, however, he retained his place in the seniors for the resumption of the Home Championship at Hampden on 9 April. But, ahead of this supposed date with destiny, Joe would do well to go to Gordon Marshall, a fellow Scot playing for England, to get a flavour of what to expect.

"Back then, your nationality was judged solely on where you were born, not on whether your mother once had a wee dance with an Englishman," says the former Hearts goalkeeper, whose son, Gordon Jnr, was capped for Scotland. "Today, Joe and I would have been eligible to play for Scotland as well, but it was something unusual to be picked for England, especially as we were both playing for Edinburgh clubs. I was very similar to Joe in that I only spent the first few weeks of my life down in England before my family returned north. I actually got picked for Scotland for an earlier Under-23 match until the Scottish Football Association realised they'd made a mistake. I was playing golf in East Lothian with Hearts. The lads came in and said, 'Congratulations, Big Man, you've just been capped.' I said, 'No, I cannie play for Scotland, I'm English. I was born in England.' The SFA had to go, 'Oops, quick, we need to get someone else in . . .'"

Something similar had happened to Joe only three months into his Hibs career, with newspapers reporting that, having watched him bag a hat-trick against Spurs, Scotland's selectors were certain to pick him to play for the Under-23 match against the Netherlands the following week. Any remaining confusion among journalists, and selectors, about Joe's eligibility was soon cleared up. When the Scotland Under-23 team was announced a few days later, Alex Young of Hearts was playing at centre forward.

Marshall, whose first trip outside Scotland since his birth came when he made his Hearts debut against Newcastle when he was 17, admits that his sole appearance for the England Under-23s was a bittersweet experience. "I got emptied because we drew 4-4 and I had a disaster," he says. "I messed it up at Ibrox. Well, Denis Law messed it up for me – the bugger! He was absolutely brilliant and tore us to shreds. He was playing against Maurice Setters and Maurice couldn't handle him.

"I actually thought England would've murdered Scotland. We had Jimmy Greaves, who scored a hat-trick, George Eastham, Bobby Charlton, George Cohen. I thought, 'I'll have nothing to do here', but, when I look at that Scottish team on paper, by Jove they had some players too: Denis Law, John White, Alan Cousins, Billy Higgins, Ian St John. There was a hell of a standard of players on that park, I was just glad to be a part of it.

"Joe was supposed to be playing that night but Charlton was playing at centre-forward instead. He played very deep. You would have the ball and you'd be looking upfield for the centre-forward and he was back. It was a great experience but I struggled a bit because I couldn't understand the language half the time. They couldn't understand me either. Joe was a wee bit more outward-going than I was. It was a funny feeling being English. I felt very proud to be on the pitch, but the anthems didn't mean much to me then. The hardest bit was trying to be one of the boys and I found that quite hard."

Although Joe denied that he was having trouble fitting in with the England squad, Terence Elliot of *The Daily Express* was adamant that the striker's Scottish accent grated with his team-mates. Under the screaming headline, "ENGLAND WON'T GIVE IT TO JOE!" Elliot's report on England's practice match against Bolton Wanderers said: "It seemed to me that the only thing some of the England players were practising was starving Joe of the ball. Could it be that a few of the ten Football League players resent Baker as an international interloper? There will be no Hampden Park goals before his ain folk unless England drop this cold-shoulder approach."

Elliot went on to cite wingers Bobby Charlton and John Connelly as "chief blind-to-Baker players", while Walter Winterbottom retorted that: "These boys must be allowed to show their individual skills."

The lack of service didn't stop Joe scoring from one of the two passes he received during the game, courtesy of Wolves' Peter Broadbent, but trying to score against Scotland would be a different proposition entirely, not least because there would be 130,000 supporters at Hampden.

Having beaten Northern Ireland during the week, Wales topped the Home Championship with four points, with England and Scotland tied on three points apiece. This meant that a victory for either side would seal the title, whereas, with goal difference counting for nothing, a draw would see the Championship shared between the three nations. The home side's chances appeared to diminish significantly in the build-up to the match, when title-chasing Spurs, rather unsportingly in the eyes of Scotland supporters, had "done a Hibs" and refused to release three of Scotland's star players: Dave Mackay, John White and goalkeeper Billy Brown.

All three would win the historic League and Cup double with Spurs the following season. At the time, Scotland were blessed with an abundance of supreme outfield talent, but with Rangers goalkeeper George Niven injured, third-choice goalkeeper Frank Haffey was given the job of keeping Joe and Charlton at bay. The story of the match was the fact that, with the whole of England and Scotland from which to choose, both sides had elected to play young lads from Motherwell at centre-forward. Although yet to score at international level, Ian St John, still playing for his home town club, was earning his fourth cap for his country.

Joe, trying to add to the international account he had opened against Northern Ireland back in November, found that the Scotland crowd at Hampden was even less enthusiastic about his appearance than some of the England supporters had initially been about his debut at Wembley. He said later: "There I was standing during the national anthem in a white shirt with the crowd roaring, 'Get back to England, you Sassenach.' I played for Hibs and lived 12 miles away!" He added: "They roasted me. To them I was an English so-and-so if I was wearing the white shirt. I took some stick, I tell you."

Denis Law, who at the time was still with Huddersfield Town, laughs at the thought. "We don't let it go do we?" he says. "Joe spoke better Scottish than me. You could never meet an Englishman with a better Scottish accent than that but, even when we were team-mates at Torino, there was always a sort of 'I'm Scottish, you're English' battle going on." Gerry adds: "Yes, he was booed, but nothing bothered him. You could set Joe on fire and it wouldn't bother him."

Despite the feverish build-up to renew the world's oldest footballing rivalry, however, the match turned out to be, in the uncompromising words of *The Scotsman's* Hugh McIlvanney, "One of the worst internationals in the history of British football." He placed much of the blame on the referee, Jeno Szranko of Hungary who, he said, "evidently saw football as much more of a gentle art than a contact sport".

At no time was this more evident than when, barely 60 seconds after Fulham's Graham Leggat had put Scotland 1-0 up in the 16th minute, Joe thought he had equalised when he charged Haffey and headed the ball out of the goalkeeper's hands. Joe appealed fervently but his effort was disallowed, with even McIlvanney agreeing that an equaliser should have been given.

Alex Young, who was making his Scotland debut, reveals that Joe wasn't the only target for the Hampden crowd. "The Scotland fans gave us a hammering because we just couldn't score," he says. "Ian St John was clean through on goal three times and missed every one. Normally he was a good, strong player."

Lamenting "the most feeble English side in living memory", a completely unbiased McIlvanney wrote: "Baker alone among their forwards had the intelligence and technique associated with the England attacks that have devastated Scottish defences during the last two decades."

He also took great exception to the "opportunist" Charlton who, when tackled by Celtic's Duncan Mackay on 49 minutes, "collapsed with theatrical thoroughness, like a character who had swallowed poison in the third act of a Victorian melodrama" to earn England an equaliser from the penalty spot.

It was clear to Young that, even though he was playing against Scotland, Joe wasn't holding back. "You could see how hard he was trying, going in for headers and trying to win the ball all the time," he says. With quarter of an hour remaining, Joe broke clear on goal with only Haffey to beat, only for Scotland captain Bobby Evans to handle the ball at his feet and give England the chance to win the game with a second penalty. "If the chance had arisen, I'd have taken it," Joe said later, "but I'm not saying if I'd have scored or sent the ball into Aikenhead Road."

In the end, the responsibility of trying to earn England both points and, with them, the British Championship, fell to Charlton. After Haffey had saved the Manchester United player's spot kick, the fastidious Szranko ordered a retake, only for Charlton to blast his second effort wide.

"I think that was when Bobby started tearing his hair out," joked Jimmy Greaves, the man who, exactly a year later, would torment Haffey during the goalkeeper's second and final appearance for Scotland – in the 9-3 demolition at Wembley.

All in all, Joe's first game for England on Scottish soil was a disappointing affair for nearly all concerned. Equally disappointing was Hibs' seventh-place finish in the league, especially as their impressive haul of 106 goals was even better than the 102 scored by champions Hearts. Joe's end-of-season tally of 42 remains a Hibs record and has been matched by only one player in the Scottish top-flight since – Third Lanark's Alex Harley, later of Manchester City, the very next season.

England's next game would be against Yugoslavia at Wembley on 11 May, before which they were scheduled to take on the England Under-23s at Highbury on the sixth, in a fixture that served as the traditional curtain-raiser to the FA Cup final. The selectors would announce the team, plus an additional six reserves, on 20 April. The squad would then take part in the England tour to Spain and Hungary. The only question was whether Hibs, with Spurs having just set the precedent of making players unavailable for international selection, would allow Joe to play. After all, Joe was the club's crowd-puller and they had their own summer tour of the Continent to consider. This would kick off with a match in Portsmouth on the same day that England were scheduled to play their young counterparts.

In the end, with newspapers speculating that Joe would demand a transfer if Hibs were to stand in the way of his international future, the Edinburgh club relented. It was bad news for Brian Clough, who might have considered himself in with a chance of another call-up had Hibs' answer been different.

Joe was one of the few positives during England's 2-1 victory over the Under-23s, scoring both goals in the first half. Despite some calls for the entire England team to be replaced following their woeful display in Glasgow, only four changes were made for the visit of Yugoslavia, a strong side who, later in the summer, would be crowned both Olympic gold-medallists and European Championship runners-up.

Arguably the biggest surprise was the omission of veteran Wolves defender Bill Slater, who had recently been named Footballer of the Year by the Football Writers' Association, in favour of Peter Swan of Sheffield Wednesday. Other changes saw Jimmy Greaves replace Ray Parry, Bryan Douglas (Blackburn) coming in for John Connelly and Peter Broadbent losing his place to Johnny Haynes (Fulham).

The 3-3 draw, played before 60,000 at Wembley, less than half the crowd at Hampden, saw Joe play a part in each of England's goals. He headed the ball into Douglas's path for the first England equaliser and played a one-two with Greaves to put the home side 2-1 up just after half-time.

After the Yugoslavs had gone into a 3-2 lead, Joe's header against the bar in the final minute rebounded for Haynes to nod home the last goal of the game. In the dying seconds, Joe had a chance to secure the win but his header hit the post.

Despite securing the draw, it was a far from convincing England performance. The friendly against Spain at Real Madrid's Bernabeu stadium four days later saw more tinkering with the line-up, with captain Ronnie Clayton being dropped in favour of Bobby Robson. But the return of the future England manager, making his first international appearance since the 1958 World Cup, and Chelsea's Peter Brabrook replacing Douglas did nothing to stop the relentless march of the Spanish, who ran out 3-0 winners. Nor was

Joe, or any of his England team-mates, able to do anything about Florian "The Emperor" Albert, who inspired Hungary to a 2-0 win in Budapest on 22 May.

Five appearances, one goal – not the kind of statistics the footballing public was used to seeing in a sentence about Joe Baker. But it was obvious to anyone that England, as a unit, were struggling. The fact that the great Bobby Charlton, who would become his nation's all-time leading goalscorer, had found the net just once – from the penalty spot – in four of those matches told its own story.

His first season as a full international may not have gone to plan but, when the new season kicked off, Joe wasted no time in showing the same kind of form that had led to his record-breaking efforts of 1959-60. After scoring in an Edinburgh Select charity match win over Chelsea, he hit four in Hibs' 6-1 League Cup victory over Airdrie. It wasn't long before Joe's attention again turned to the international calendar, with England Under-23 selectors facing something of a crisis ahead of their next fixture, against East Germany at Maine Road on 21 September. A series of clashes with midweek English League fixtures meant that a number of players, including Jimmy Greaves, Peter Bonetti and Terry Venables of Chelsea, and Alan Mullery and Tony Macedo of Fulham, would be unable to represent their country.

The absence of Macedo and Bonetti opened up the way for Leicester City's Gordon Banks to make his debut, while Bobby Moore and Brian Labone would also be appearing in an England shirt for the first time. But only four days before the match was due to kick off, East Germany announced that they would be unable to fulfil the fixture due to the escalating problems in Berlin, which would subsequently lead to the construction of the Berlin Wall the following year. A hastily assembled Danish XI stepped in as a replacement, including several members of the summer's Olympic Games silver medal-winning squad. With the match not counted as an official Under-23 international, Joe opened the scoring in a 5-1 win, with Bobby Charlton (two), Moore and Southampton's Terry Paine getting the others.

But, come 26 September, the thought of missing out on an official Under-23 cap was the least of Joe's worries. This was the day, with Hibs sitting second bottom of the league without a single point, when Joe found out he had been dropped by England. He had led the line for nearly a year in five consecutive internationals but, in the Home Championship match against Northern Ireland on 8 October, it would be Bobby Smith of Spurs who would be wearing the No. 9 shirt.

With 13 league goals for the season already, nobody could deny that 27-year-old Smith was worthy of his first England cap. He had, after all, gone to the 1958 World Cup in Sweden and not stepped on the pitch. Stung as he was, Joe tried to stay upbeat. He was still only 20 and other opportunities to wear the England shirt surely wouldn't be far away. He also insisted that, despite his club's struggling form, he would be staying at Hibs. On reports that Wolves manager Stan Cullis was prepared to spend big to bring him to Molineux, Joe commented: "I'm still happy with Hibs even though I have lost my England place. I certainly shall not ask for a transfer."

Such a move may have appeared attractive, however, when Hibs suffered their eighth consecutive league defeat, leaving them propping up the table. Joe finally had something to celebrate again when he was selected to play for the England Under-23s against Italy at Newcastle's St James' Park on 2 November. After Juventus star Bruno Nicole had put the young Italians ahead after only six minutes, Joe equalised shortly afterwards, but in controversial circumstances.

The use of the shoulder-charge on goalkeepers had been in the spotlight in recent years, with Manchester United being on the receiving end in both the 1957 and 1958 FA Cup finals. After only six minutes of the 1957 contest, Aston Villa's Peter McParland clattered into Ray Wood with such ferocity that the goalkeeper was knocked unconscious and broke his jaw. He was forced to spend the vast majority of the match as a virtual outfield passenger as McParland struck twice against makeshift goalkeeper Jackie Blanchflower to give Villa the win. Bolton legend Nat Lofthouse did something similar the following year, scoring his second goal of the game by bundling Harry Gregg into the net.

Against the young Italians, Joe claimed that his challenge on Roberto Anzolin, a future member of his country's 1966 World Cup squad, was "a fair and square shoulder-charge", but the Azzurri saw it very differently. With the goalkeeper sprawled on the turf, the furious Italians – including Giovanni Trapattoni and Gianni Rivera – surrounded the Belgian referee, urging him, in no uncertain terms, to change his mind about awarding the goal. Things quickly got out of hand, with police called on to the pitch to try to restore order. Several of the Italian players began to leave the field in disgust, before being persuaded to continue by manager Giovanni Ferrari. The Italian trainer tended to Anzolin and, having done so, kissed his fingers in disgust at the referee.

In the same way that he couldn't understand why his goal against Scotland had been disallowed, Joe was equally bemused that what he saw as a perfectly legitimate effort should cause such consternation, but it wouldn't be the last time in his career that he would be on the receiving end of Italian aggression. The unofficial match at Maine Road aside, the bad-tempered draw against the Italian Under-23s marked the first time Bobby Moore had worn an England shirt. Although he didn't know it at the time, it would be five long years before Joe would do so again.

10
Mad for It

Around the same time that Joe Baker was bundling Italian goalkeepers into the net, a surprise contender for his England place was emerging. After signing for Manchester City in a £17,000 deal on 3 November 1960, Gerry Baker announced, "I was born in New York, but I believe if I play in English football I can get a lawyer to prove I am eligible for England. After all, my father was an Englishman, and if I can qualify for this country I want to put that fellow Joe Baker out of the England team."

Today, Gerry insists this was a joke, and that he had no burning desire to oust his brother from the England line-up. His main reason for leaving St Mirren, he says, was the chance to play alongside Denis Law and that "I would far rather have Jackie Plenderleith playing behind me than against me".

So prolific up until now, the 1960-61 season had started in less than spectacular fashion for Gerry. By the time of his transfer, he had scored only one goal in five appearances in the League Cup and two goals in nine outings in the league. Only one team was below St Mirren in the table – Joe's Hibs, whose first points of the season came in Gerry's last appearance for the Saints. Unlike his brother, Gerry scored in the game, which finished 4-3 to Hibs at Easter Road.

The occasions on which the brothers were scheduled to play against each other at least meant that there was one less difficult decision to be made in the Baker household. Gerry recalls: "On match days, our mum would cook us the best fillet steaks – 'You've got to feed footballers well,' she used to say. Over lunch, she would look to me, then she would look across at Joe and say, 'I wonder where I'll go today.' Joe and I would be looking down at our food, hoping that it wouldn't be us that she would come and watch. If she said, 'I'll just go and watch Gerry,' I'd be mumbling, 'For fuck's sake.' Her brothers had played football so she knew the game – she loved it. When I got home after a match, she'd be saying 'Why didn't you do this, why didn't you do that?' and I would be trying to argue with her, but there was no point. If she'd been to see Joe play, he would stop her in her tracks by telling her, 'Mammy, I've got ten directors, two managers and 99 coaches telling me how I should play. I don't need you trying to tell me as well, so shoosh!'"

Lizzie also got little joy from her younger son when she tried to ask him about his adventures abroad. "Joe won't talk when he comes home from some of those interesting trips that he goes on with the teams," she said. "I'm always dying to know all about everything – what the food was like, were the hotels good, how did the places look. But all I get out of that boy is 'It was all right, Mammy.' He never tells me anything, just shrugs his shoulders and says everything was all right."

As well as taking in her boys' matches live, "Ma" Baker also followed her sons' careers avidly via radio and television reports. "The first time I saw, and heard, Joe on television I gave him a row when he came home," she said. "His accent was *terrible*. I said I thought he might have tried to talk a bit more politely, but Joe said it didn't matter and that was the way they wanted him to talk anyway. I will tell you, you can't tell boys anything if you're their mother."

As much as he loved and was devoted to the woman who brought him into the world, the move out of the family home he also shared with Joe, stepfather David Houborn and younger stepbrothers John and Robert, was something of a relief to Gerry, who became engaged to his long-term girlfriend, local lass Anne Stevenson, shortly after joining St Mirren.

Manchester City's Paisley-born manager Les McDowall, on the hunt for a goalscorer who could take full advantage of the magic of the recently signed Denis Law, had first approached St Mirren regarding Gerry in late September. This was met with a wholly unambiguous reply from Buddies' boss Willie Reid, who announced: "Baker is not for sale", while Gerry himself added: "I have had experience of football in England, and since coming back to Scotland I have never wanted to return south."

Like the fans of today, however, St Mirren's followers soon realised that public statements from football clubs and their actual intentions are not necessarily one and the same. Just over a month later, Gerry became the fifth member of the 1959 Scottish Cup-winning team to leave Love Street.

"I was told Manchester City wanted to sign me after I had finished training yesterday morning," Gerry told *The Daily Mail* on the day of his transfer. "As far as I was concerned, this was my big chance. I jumped at it. I had no time to tell my fiancée that we are likely to begin our married life in Manchester. I left my mother to break that piece of news."

Within 20 minutes of arriving by train in Manchester, Gerry had signed for City, but had to wait for another hour to see if defender John McTavish would agree to return to Scotland as part of the deal. When all the paperwork had been completed, including McTavish signing for St Mirren,

City announced that Gerry would be making his debut away to Bolton Wanderers in two days' time.

"Where's Bolton? It's near London isn't it?" joked Gerry. "I want to get back to Scotland quickly after the game if I can, to have a long talk with my fiancée – to tell her about my new club." Asked by the *Daily Mail's* Frank Taylor whether he had misplaced his shooting boots of late, Gerry replied: "I hope not. I seem to be hitting the post an awful lot for St Mirren, but with City I aim to start finding the net again. With chaps like Denis Law and George Hannah alongside me I know I'll have plenty of chances."

Looking back over old interviews, Gerry's jovial attitude will be familiar to nearly everyone who has known him. The overriding memory of those who played with him at Manchester City, including Denis Law, who referred to him as a "Jack the lad", is that of a young man with a happy-go-lucky, almost carefree attitude to football and to life. But the poignancy of a visit to the tailor to collect his club blazer wasn't lost on the then 22-year-old.

Two and half years before Gerry signed for City, football was mourning the loss of eight members of Manchester United's Busby Babes in the Munich Air Disaster, not to mention the 15 other fatalities, including former Manchester City goalkeeper Frank Swift. While Matt Busby, Bobby Charlton and other survivors were in the midst of rebuilding the shattered Old Trafford club, the fallout still cast a large shadow over the city.

"I remember seeing all these Manchester United blazers hanging up in the shop," recalls Gerry. "The tailor told me that they belonged to the lads who didn't make it back from Germany. Seeing something like that puts a lot of things into perspective."

Gerry went straight into the Manchester City side to play Bolton, wearing the unfamiliar No.10 shirt. This, explains former City reserve player Fred Eyre, dated back to Don Revie's time at the club.

On their way to the 1955 FA Cup final, Les McDowall, influenced by the Magical Magyars of Hungary, had deployed Revie as a deep-lying centre-forward who would draw the opposing centre-backs out of position. Although City lost the Cup final to Newcastle, the "Revie Plan" proved a success the following season, when they won the final against Birmingham.

"It was four years later and Revie was long gone, but we were still trying to play the same way," says Eyre, who turned his frustration of never making a first-team appearance for his beloved City into a bestselling book: *Kicked into Touch*. "So while Gerry was an out-and-out striker, at first he didn't wear No.9 because that was the number worn by our playmaker, little George Hannah. He played in a withdrawn role with Gerry and

Law as the two spearheads. It's quite normal today but, back then, it was revolutionary."

Revolutionary tactics or not, Gerry's Manchester City career got off to a poor start. He came close to scoring on his debut, hitting the underside of the bar, but Nat Lofthouse, in one of his final games for the Trotters, inspired Bolton to a 3-1 win.

After defeat at home to West Ham, Gerry scored his first goal in English football away to former club Chelsea, but it made little difference as City lost 6-3. Three more defeats followed, with Gerry finding the net in a 4-2 home reverse against Wolves, before the new signing got his first taste of victory in a sky blue shirt.

"To be honest, we weren't a good side," admits Eyre, who at the time was a 16-year-old apprentice. "Gerry's signing was big news, City buying this prolific goalscorer from Scotland, but he arrived into a poor team."

Gerry admitted afterwards: "I found it hard to get going at Maine Road. The marking and covering were much tighter. There are some Scots who, having gone to England, say the game there is much faster, but I feel the main difference is that the English have more full-time, fully trained players. And then there was the mud…"

After six defeats in a row, City had slumped to 14th place, but Gerry was able to give the home support some festive cheer when his Christmas Eve brace against Fulham secured a 3-2 win. It was perhaps no coincidence that, for the first time in his fledgling Manchester City career, Gerry was wearing the No.9 shirt. But it is for his sparkling personality off the field, rather than his performances on it, that Gerry is most fondly remembered by his former team-mates.

"Gerry wasn't just a good goalscorer, he was a great guy and a great character," says Law. "He had a terrific sense of humour."

"The first thing that comes into my mind whenever anyone mentions Gerry Baker is that he always seemed to be smiling or laughing," adds Eyre. "From the minute he walked through the door, you could tell he had such a bright and breezy personality. Everybody loved him and he was great with the kids, like me and Neil Young. I used to have to clean his boots. I don't know what size he took but, for the size of him, I always thought he had big boots, but I don't know whether that's only my imagination!

"Manchester was the place to be in the early Sixties. I know Liverpool had The Beatles, but they played loads of gigs up at the Oasis in Manchester. It was a fantastic place to be. Every lunchtime we all went to the Plaza. Gerry was there as soon as he came down. There was an amusement arcade – he spent a lot of time in there as well. It was very handy because he could go from the Plaza to the amusement arcade and never get wet. He settled in straight away. Everyone loved him. He was a really good lad."

Former City winger Roy Cheetham adds: "Gerry mixed and settled down very well. He liked his nightlife and made sure he found out where all the best nightclubs were, but it didn't seem to affect his game because he was a very good player."

"The club scene in Manchester was fantastic," admits Gerry. "And it was even better because most of the bouncers seemed to be Manchester City supporters. The football club were great as well. They gave Anne and I our first house together, in Dalmorton Road. Matt Busby lived just around the corner."

Gerry and Anne married back home in Viewpark, Motherwell, in January 1961, with the local priest almost jumping the gun when it came to the tradition of a jilted bride marrying the best man. "He was very old and he turned to Joe and said, 'Do you, Joseph, take Anne . . .' Joe had to say, 'No, Father, it's Gerry that's getting married!'"

The couple's first daughter, Karen, was born on 12 August. Before then, however, Gerry had to contend with some further, sometimes painful, frustration on the football field. After scoring the winner in a 2-1 victory over Everton at Maine Road, he was dropped following a 4-1 defeat at Blackburn. In his next match, he was playing for the reserves against Derby County – and it wasn't just his pride that took a battering at the Baseball Ground.

"I can still see it now," says Fred Eyre, in his unmistakable Mancunian accent. "Paddy Fagan, who had recently been transferred from City, was chasing a ball down the left. I don't know why Gerry wasn't down the field on this occasion, but Paddy took the ball down to the corner flag and Gerry was right behind him, snapping at his heels – 'Snap, snap, snap.' Paddy left the ball, stopped, turned round and smacked Gerry right in the kisser. He didn't wait for the referee – he just walked off. Paddy was 5ft 5 inches tall and the nicest bloke you could ever hope to meet. I think he was frustrated, like Gerry would have been, at finding himself in the reserves. But in a 15-year career that took in Hull City, Manchester City, Derby County and the Republic of Ireland, that was the one and only time Paddy ever got sent off – for punching Gerry Baker right in the fuckin' teeth."

Fagan laughs, describing the incident as "a difference of opinion". Gerry's bruised chin, and his exile, didn't last long, and he was back in the first team for the remainder of the season. His brace in a 2-1 win at Leicester City in the penultimate match brought his league tally to nine goals in 22 matches.

"He wasn't the type of player to score 20-yard screamers – within the six-yard box and 18-yard box was his speciality," says Eyre. "I can't remember him scoring any spectacular goals, but I'd have been more than happy to score any one of his. Gerry wasn't big so he wasn't beating centre halves in the air, but anything that came across the box which, in that poorish side, wasn't a lot, he was always in and around, unsettling defenders and trying to get on the end of stuff. I'm sure he'd love to have played in a better team, but it wasn't one of our strongest eras – even though we had Gerry, who was fantastic, we had Bert Trautmann in goal and we had Law, who was like nothing you've ever seen in your life."

Sadly for City supporters, they didn't have Law for much longer. During the summer, he was transferred to Torino for £110,000 – a record fee between British and Italian clubs. The detrimental impact of the Scotsman's departure wasn't immediate. As a replacement, City signed Peter Dobing, Joe Baker's team-mate at Under-23 level, from Blackburn. Thanks to three goals from Dobing, four from Joe Hayes, and another three from Gerry, City topped the table in early September, with five wins from six matches.

After pulling a muscle against Everton, Gerry missed the next match – a 3-0 defeat away to Arsenal. He scored on his return, a 2-1 win over Bolton, and again in a 2-2 draw with West Bromwich Albion with what would turn out to be his last competitive goal in English football for more than two years.

After a promising start to the 1961-62 season, a series of poor results saw Manchester City begin to slip down the table. But Gerry, at least, had something to look forward to on 11 October. As part of the deal that saw Denis Law transferred to Italy, Torino had agreed to play a friendly at Maine Road. And the Lawman wouldn't be the only familiar face in the opposition line-up.

11
Beautiful Horizon

In the aftermath of the Second World War, as Europe lay smouldering and Britain faced up to financial hardship, an Austrian opera impresario proposed that he would "provide a platform for the flowering of the human spirit" by staging a multicultural music festival in Britain. Rudolf Bing's first choice of host city was Oxford but, after negotiations fell through, Edinburgh stepped forward. Today, the capital of Scotland plays host to the world's largest arts festival. During the month of August, thousands flock to the city as it becomes a sea of theatre, culture and third-rate comedians shoving flyers under the noses of unsuspecting tourists. But Bing and the rest of the Festival's founding fathers could not have known that their decision to choose Edinburgh as the host city would lead indirectly to one of Hibs' most memorable footballing achievements.

Despite not being – strictly speaking – a trade fair, the Edinburgh International Festival was deemed a good enough reason for the club to be invited to compete in the 1960-61 Inter-Cities Fairs Cup. Hibs had already made history in 1955-56 when they became the first British side to compete in the European Cup, playing their first game in the same week that Joe Baker was taking part in a trial match. Hibs memorably reached the semi-finals and now, with Joe as their star player, they were set to become the first Scottish side to take part in the Fairs Cup. The competition was being held for only the third time, and this would be the first to be played over the course of a single season.

In the first round, Hibs were paired with Lausanne Sport, but Joe's first taste of European football would have to wait as the Swiss side withdrew from the competition without a ball being kicked. Hibs were awarded a 2-0 win. Realistically, the quarter-finals would be as far as Hugh Shaw's side would go as, on 14 December, they were scheduled to welcome Barcelona to Easter Road. Not only were the giants of Catalonia the only side to have won the Fairs Cup but, a month earlier, they had knocked Real Madrid out of the European Cup – a competition their fierce rivals had won in such devastating fashion in Glasgow earlier in the year. Facing Barcelona was a daunting task for Hibs, even more so when fog rolled in over Leith, forcing the match to be postponed. The tie was turned on its head, with the scheduled second leg in the Nou Camp on 27 December becoming Hibs' first match of the competition.

"We were complete underdogs," admits John Fraser. "Barcelona were then what they are now – probably the best team in Europe, near enough the world. Half the team were the Hungarians that beat England 7-1 and we were very much outsiders."

Aside from Luis Suarez, the recently crowned European Footballer of the Year, another of Barcelona's biggest stars was Sandor Kocsis. Even at 31, "the man with the golden head", who scored 75 goals in only 68 internationals for Hungary, was a fearsome opponent, boasting a record that put even Joe Baker in the shade.

Hibs had visited the Nou Camp a year and a half earlier during a summer tour and Joe's performance, despite a 5-1 defeat, was enough to persuade Barcelona officials to make a big-money offer for the striker. The attendance for the Fairs Cup tie was 60,000 – the capacity of the Nou Camp ahead of its expansion. This was three times the number of supporters who turned out for the 1959 friendly, but there was little to suggest that the scoreline would be much different. On the day of the match, Barcelona, the reigning champions of Spain, were second in La Liga, while Hibs sat 16th in the Scottish First Division, three points above bottom club St Mirren.

There were some slender signs of hope, however. Just before Christmas, Hibs, and Joe in particular, had enjoyed the perfect warm-up to the big game by hammering Third Lanark 8-4 at Easter Road. Joe scored five times, but the chances of him adding to his tally in Barcelona still appeared remote.

It was certainly a surprise to fans in the Nou Camp, if not to Joe himself, when he shot Hibs into the lead after only seven minutes. There was further Catalonian consternation 11 minutes later, when Johnny MacLeod made it 2-0. Joe and MacLeod would later repeat their European heroics while playing together at Arsenal, but Kocsis restored a sense of reality to the situation with goals in the 38th and 53rd minutes. But, far from caving in, Hibs did the unthinkable and restored their two-goal advantage with a strike from Tom Preston in the 72nd minute and another from Joe in the 74th. "We couldn't believe the way the game was going," says Fraser, while Preston neatly sums up exactly how it felt to be 4-2 up at the Nou Camp with the seconds ticking away: "We thought, 'Oh Christ!'"

The inside-forward had every reason to be nervous, especially with Kocsis on the field. The great Hungarian completed his hat-trick with only seven minutes remaining, before Brazilian Macedo equalised at the death. The final score of 4-4 is something that Hibs would happily have taken before the match but, under the circumstances, it was a bit of a disappointment, particularly when away goals counted for nothing. It had been an heroic effort from the Hibs players, especially Joe. A Barcelona official admitted afterwards that the club had "missed the boat" when they failed to sign him the previous year. The player's value, and his importance to Hibs, was increasing exponentially. By the time the fiercely anticipated second leg took place on 22 February 1961, Joe had not only helped to haul his club midway up the league table, but he had also come painfully close to emulating his brother's incredible Scottish Cup scoring feat of a year earlier.

Drawn at home against non-league Peebles Rovers, Joe scored nine goals in a 15-1 win. And, reveals Tom Preston, the score could have been higher had it not been for Joe's team-mates doing their best to help him emulate, or even eclipse, Gerry's heroics against Glasgow University.

"I was getting dog's abuse from the punters because Joe had scored nine and I was trying to get him to score ten," says Preston. "I could've scored goals myself but I kept giving the ball to Joe to see if he could get the tenth goal! It was that easy."

For the first time in his career, Joe even assumed penalty duties to boost his personal goal count. "When he 'only' got nine, I was like, 'YES!'" laughs Gerry. "Joe told me he missed a chance deliberately, I said 'You're a liar!'"

The result saw Hibs' odds of winning the Scottish Cup slashed from 20-1 to 7-2, making them second favourites behind Rangers. But before travelling to Douglas Park to face Hamilton in the next round, there was the small matter of Barcelona's visit to Leith to consider. The opposition had shuffled their pack since the first game, dropping three players, while Bobby Kinloch came in for Hibs at inside-left. "Losing would have been a complete disaster for Barcelona," says Fraser.

A crowd of 50,000 packed into Easter Road for the Wednesday night game and this time Joe kept them waiting, not heading Hibs into the lead until ten minutes into the match. Eulogio Martinez, the Paraguayan striker, headed an equaliser with half an hour gone before – for the first time in the tie – Kocsis put Barcelona ahead just before half-time.

Hibs came out strongly after the break and forced an equaliser through Preston. The match looked to be heading for another draw when Johannes Malka, the German referee, took centre stage. Joe played the ball through to MacLeod, who fell under the tackle of Spanish international defender Enric Gensana. Malka immediately pointed to the spot, a decision which, predictably, the Barcelona players politely queried.

The Herald's match report states: "The award seemed somewhat harsh. To a man the Spaniards protested, chased the referee into the Hibernian half of the field and back again to their own 18-yard line; he was pushed and buffeted, tripped, kicked, and twice struck on the chest by gesticulating fists. The police, patrolling the track, joined in the fray and their Scottish phlegm was never more needed than in their efforts to calm the Barcelona team, whose officials also pled for order."

When some kind of order was restored several minutes later, the responsibility of taking the all-important spot kick fell on the shoulders of Bobby Kinloch. Sammy Baird was the regular penalty taker but was forced to relinquish his duties on the night because, as was delicately revealed by Kinloch during a 2008 interview, the Hibs captain "had shat himself". In a moment that guaranteed him legendary status at Easter Road, Kinloch blasted the ball past teenage goalkeeper Carlos Medrano. The ground erupted, in more ways than one.

"When it was getting near time up, the referee waited until he was right on the halfway line, near the stand, before he blew the full-time whistle," recalls Fraser. "He blew the whistle and then ran for it. The Barcelona players chased him up the tunnel. He managed to shut himself away in the referee's room and for years afterwards the marks were still on the door from where the players were kicking and scraping their boots down it. For years afterwards, showing people the marks on the door was part and parcel of the Easter Road stadium tour. Barcelona didn't like the decision, and they certainly didn't like being beaten."

The mood of Barcelona's players would be little better come the end of the season, after losing the European Cup final to Benfica and finishing 20 points behind Real Madrid in the league.

For Hibs, victory meant their second European semi-final in succession, while the experience had proved a memorable introduction to Continental competition for Joe. That weekend, he helped his side ease past Hamilton, 4-0, to set up a last-eight meeting with Celtic in the Scottish Cup. The last time they had beaten Celtic in a Scottish Cup tie was in the final of 1902, incidentally the last time that Hibs had got their hands on the trophy. Unfortunately for Hibs fans, things stayed true to form. Not even knocking the mighty Barcelona out of Europe gave them the impetus to break the Cup hoodoo, with Celtic triumphing after a replay.

Still a reasonably respectable seventh in the league, Hibs' only possibility of silverware was in the Fairs Cup, in which they would be up against Roma for a place in the final. On 19 April, the same evening that Rangers reached the final of the European Cup Winners' Cup at the expense of Wolves, Hibs were attempting to make it a Scottish European double, although they were somewhat fortunate that the match ended in a 2-2 draw.

MacLeod equalised with a late free-kick after Joe had cancelled out the first of Francisco Lojacono's two strikes.

By this stage, of course, officials at the Italian club would have to be living in a cave beneath the Colosseum not to be aware of the threat posed by Joe. But Eddie Turnbull, now a coach at Easter Road, devised a cunning strategy in order to conquer the Italians in the second leg.

"Eddie Turnbull decided that he would put the No.9 jersey on me and called me Joe Baker," reveals Kinloch, "and they put the No.8 on Joe and called him Bobby Kinloch. They ended up watching me while Joe did the other bits and pieces. They weren't paying as much attention to him because Bobby Kinloch was rubbish! The classic thing about it was that I actually scored in that game while they thought I was Joe Baker."

With a strike that would have secured victory under the away goals rule, Joe (aka Bobby) scored his second goal late on to secure a 3-3 draw. After 180 minutes and five goals apiece, there was still no separating the two sides. The protracted tie was decided in emphatic fashion a month later, during a play-off in Rome. While Rangers were losing the second leg of their Cup Winners' Cup final in Florence, Hibs were being trounced 6-0 at the Stadio Olympico. What made matters worse was the fact that Third Lanark had also hit them for six in the final league match of the season a few weeks earlier.

Pedro Manfredini, Roma's Argentinian striker, grabbed four of his side's goals. But there was a far bigger, almost unthinkable, story behind Hibs' comprehensive defeat in Italy. Joe Baker, their star player, the crowd puller, and the striker who, still not 21 years old, had scored 141 goals in only 160 appearances, had already signed for another club.

12
Raging Bull

Joe Baker and Denis Law went to Italy for the money. It was that simple, and it's a refreshing response to the question of why Law quit Manchester City in favour of Torino. In carefully worded PR statements, the football superstars of today insist that they rejected a £100,000-a-week offer from one club in favour of £120,000 a week from another because they "want to win trophies", they "feel it's time to move on" or, that perennial favourite, because Barcelona/Manchester United/Queens Park Rangers are "a massive club". The fact a new contract means a player can now afford to put an extra wing on his mock Tudor mansion is the solid gold elephant in the room.

Law, who was earning the English maximum of £20 a week at Manchester City when he left the club in the summer of 1961, sees no need to put a spin on his response. "Joe and I didn't go to Italy for the sun, the quality of football or anything else," says the Scotland legend. "It was purely for the money. We are Scottish after all, although Joe was born in England, he was really Scottish in a way. The basic wages in England and Scotland were about £20 a week. In Italy you were talking about £100-£200 a week, which at that time was enormous."

Although Law played alongside Gerry at Manchester City, it wasn't by design that he and Joe ended up in Turin at the same time. Joe's outstanding performances for Hibs, particularly those in Europe, during the 1960-61 season, had attracted considerable attention from the Continent, with Barcelona and Fiorentina among the clubs reportedly vying for his signature. Joe admitted that he had no desire to leave Hibs, his "first love", but for all his brilliance in front of goal, he was still earning only £12 a week. He had tried to supplement this modest income. Ahead of the England tour the previous summer, he had fixed himself up with Bagenal Harvey, the same London-based agent who put England skipper Johnny Haynes and cricketer Denis Compton on Brylcreem billboards up and down the land. One of Joe's first deals was with an electric razor company. All he needed to do to collect his fee was grow a beard and then shave it off in front of the television cameras. There was just one problem: Joe couldn't grow a beard. Even after going weeks without shaving, nobody had really noticed a difference. He also appeared with a number of other footballers in a short film sponsored by the Scottish Co-operative Wholesale Society. Directed by Enrico Cocozza, later described as "Wishaw's answer to David Lynch", *Meet the Stars* shows Joe demonstrating his skills alongside the likes of Celtic's Bertie Peacock and Alex Scott of Rangers. It also shows Third Lanark goalkeeper Jocky Robertson taking a break between the sticks to spark up a Rocky Mount cigarette.

So Joe had the stardom, he had an England career, albeit one on hold, he had a beautiful girlfriend in the shape of Sonia Haughey, a 17-year-old Scots-Italian girl from Wishaw, he had a column in the *Daily Record* – he even had an invitation to the BBC's Sports Personality of the Year Award.

What he also had, much to his chagrin, was an employer who was still paying him a comparative pittance. "I was on close to £18 a week, a lot more than Joe, and I was rubbish," says the self-effacing Bobby Kinloch. Joe would have been happy to stay at Easter Road, he explained, but his outlandish wage demands, a suggestion made to him by Willie Ormond, proved a sticking point among the Hibs hierarchy.

Joe said: "It was re-signing time and I went upstairs to talk with manager Hugh Shaw and chairman Harry Swan. They put the paper in front of me and were surprised that I should hesitate to sign. I told them I wanted a rise and the chairman inquired how much. I replied that a fiver would keep me happy, and they muttered about needing time to think about it. They didn't ponder long, for the next day the newspapers carried the story that Hibs couldn't satisfy Baker's demands. It just shows how a fiver a week could have altered the course of my career."

On 15 April 1961, when Joe would dearly have loved to be playing in England's 9-3 victory over Scotland at Wembley, he was instead at home reading the following Hibs statement: "If Baker insists on his demands, he will leave the club with no alternative but to refuse."

The row over Joe's call to be paid £18 a week simmered over the final few games of the season and, even though he was still banging in the goals, the Hibs board would not be moved. On 2 May – the same day that Ian St John left Motherwell for Liverpool in a £35,000 deal – Joe was placed on the transfer list, with Chelsea, Newcastle, Wolves, Roma, with whom Hibs were still fighting for the right to face Birmingham City in the final of the Fairs Cup, and Torino among the interested parties.

When Joe was a late stand-in for Johnny Byrne to play for the England Under-23s against the senior side at Stamford Bridge on 5 May, Roma officials flew in to see him with a view to making a £60,000 bid. Joe said: "I shall go where the money is. I know negotiations are going on between Hibs and Roma, and I'm quite prepared to play in Italy. I don't mind at all."

But Hibs, too, were waiting for the best offer and subsequently received it from Gina Giusto, the secretary of Torino. Joe's £65,000 departure from Easter Road to the north of Italy ended weeks of speculation about the striker's future. The deal was finally struck at Edinburgh's Royal British Hotel, on the world-famous Princes Street, on 11 May. Still two months shy of his 21st birthday and with Jimmy Greaves still in final discussions with AC Milan, Joe became the first British player to sign for an Italian club since John Charles swapped Leeds United for Juventus for exactly the same fee in 1957.

For a player who had been on £12 a week at Easter Road, Joe's £12,000 signing-on fee – to be paid over two years – was eye-watering. The same could be said for his lift, with soon-to-be former team-mate John Fraser picking him up in the same van he used to collect pigswill for his father's smallholding. Fraser says: "Joe got in the van carrying this big bag and I asked him what was in it – I couldn't believe it when he told me it was his signing-on fee."

Joe and Fraser played one more game together, Hibs' Fairs Cup play-off in Rome. The 6-0 defeat was an especially disappointing result for Joe as, predictably, the eyes of the Italian media were now firmly on him. The following day, he travelled north to meet again with Torino officials, taking in his new club's 2-1 victory over Catania before returning to Scotland to say his goodbyes.

Hindsight, it is said, is a wonderful thing and had Joe or Law realised what awaited them in Italy, they may well have opted to stay at home. Even more frustratingly for the pair, England's maximum wage was abolished in January 1961, with Johnny Haynes becoming England's first £100 a week footballer. "We had already made the decision to go to Italy just as the wage situation in England was changing," sighs Law.

Nevertheless, the prospect of earning £100 to £200 a week in Serie A was still hugely attractive. Law was just as excited as Joe following his own record-breaking £100,000 transfer from the City Ground, with the prospect of a fellow "Scot" for company an added bonus.

"I had been playing with Gerry in Manchester for a year and now here I was going to play alongside Joe for Torino – I couldn't get rid of the Bakers!" he laughs. "I hadn't discussed my move with Joe beforehand but I was glad he was going because I didn't want to go there on my own. But it turned out that everything about Italy was lovely apart from the football. Torino was lovely, although we thought there would be sunshine but, of course, it was at the bottom of the Alps so there was a lot of snow. The people were lovely, the food was lovely, but the football was awful. We both had an extremely difficult time in Italy. The game was completely different to what we expected. It was very defensive."

The man who engineered the move to Torino on behalf of Joe and Law was Gigi Peronace, an English-based Italian football agent. Peronace had already overseen the transfer of the great John Charles who, inadvertently, had done much to lull Serie A's newcomers into a false sense of security. The big Welshman had made life for a British striker in Italian football look so effortless, hitting 28 goals in his debut season for Juventus in 1957-58. Even Charles, however, admitted that playing in Italy would not be to everyone's taste. "The fact is that Italian League football, despite all its so-called glamour, big money and fanatical hero-worshipping crowds, is not all it is cracked up to be," he wrote in 1959. "For one thing, the atmosphere is entirely different and the tactics adopted by most teams would, I feel, bore English crowds to tears if they had to watch this kind of slow motion football week after week."

Nevertheless, the 'Gentle Giant', who in 1997 was voted by supporters as Juventus's greatest ever overseas player, would eventually score 93 goals in 155 games for the Bianconeri. As well as Joe and Law, two other strikers joined the British invasion of Serie A in 1961, all hoping to follow in Charles's considerable footsteps. Jimmy Greaves, in explosive form for struggling Chelsea, signed for AC Milan, while Aston Villa's Gerry Hitchens, who had impressed Internazionale bosses after scoring twice in England's 3-2 victory over Italy in Rome, also headed to the San Siro.

Like the transfers of Joe and Law, Greaves's move from Stamford Bridge to Milan had been facilitated by Peronace. "If a crocodile could talk it would sound like Gigi Peronace," wrote Greaves in his autobiography. "He was an imposing figure, one to be wary of, yet he could charm a bracelet." But while Hitchens, like Charles, was able to adapt to life on the continent and spend several years in Italy, no member of the young trio of Law, Greaves and Baker managed to see out their first season. In the years that followed, all three would feature on various lists of British footballers who had "flopped" abroad.

"We were too young when we went to Italy," admits Law. "We were 21, but it wasn't like someone of that age today. It was a different era and we were immature, really. I think if we'd perhaps gone two years later it might have been a different ball game altogether. We'd have been more aware of what we were going to and, of course, today, footballers playing in a different country have the media, the internet, you're not really away from your family because you've got contacts wherever you are. When me and Joe were in Turin, we were stuck there. We didn't have a phone and we could only call home once a week, so we did get a bit homesick. One saving grace was a guy called Jimmy Rodger, a sports reporter for the *Daily Record*, who used to send over a copy of the newspaper for us every day. It was fantastic as we were able to keep up with what was going on back home."

The 1961-62 campaign was only Torino's second season back in the top flight. They had been relegated to Serie B in 1959 after a decade of struggle following the tragic events of Superga – one of the darkest days in the history of Italian football. Under the dynamic leadership of Italian international captain Valentino Mazzola, *Il Grande Torino*, "The Great Torino", seemed invincible. Using a pioneering 4-2-4 system, Mazzola's men had won four successive Serie A titles and were on the verge of a fifth when, on 4 May 1949, they were returning from a friendly match in Lisbon.

Disoriented by thick cloud, the pilot of their Fiat G-212 plane descended too quickly, smashing into a wall at the back of a church on the Superga hillside, just outside Turin. The crash and resultant inferno killed all 31 people on board, including 18 members of the Grande Torino squad. Italy mourned. Replacing a group of players that included the likes of Giuseppe Grezar, Romeo Menti and Eusebio Castigliano would be impossible, re-building a team of any note would take years, but the signing of Joe and Law was seen as a step in the right direction.

As part of his transfer deal, Law's final game for Manchester City was against Joe, and his new club Torino, in Italy on 7 June. Gerry, who was in the City line-up, recalls a damp squib of an evening. "Torino's two new big stars got this big fanfare in the stadium," he says. "Then the heavens opened, we had thunder and lightning, and the match was abandoned before we'd even played half an hour."

In retrospect, it was pathetic fallacy – a sign of a storm brewing for both players. After moving to Italy, it became clear that Torino were not the only club looking overseas to boost their attack. "Most of the strikers in Italy at that time were foreign," explains Law. "They came from Argentina, Brazil, Germany, Sweden, who had a terrific national team in those days, and of course Britain. Italy was only producing defenders because that's how all the teams were playing. The attacking players weren't getting the opportunity to come through so the Serie A teams were signing strikers from abroad."

In the 12 seasons between the Superga disaster and Law and Joe's arrival in Italy, only two home-grown strikers had led the Serie A scoring charts, with Charles topping the list in 1958. Hoping for great things from their own foreign signings, the Torino supporters welcomed Joe and Law with open arms. The players got a luxury £15,000 apartment overlooking the

River Po and they were soon out sampling the city's restaurants and night-life. As young men with extra money in the bank and the football world at their feet, learning Italian wasn't at the top of the pair's list, but they would soon learn the meaning of Catenaccio – the "door-bolt" defensive system that had made the job of a Serie A striker tougher than uncooked spaghetti.

"At that particular time, Italian football was really, really defensive and we were basically playing in an 8-2 formation," says Law. "Some of the best players in Italy were goalkeepers. I don't know why, because they had nothing to do. Very often, it was a case of whoever scored the first goal won the game – that was it. Joe was a striker, I was in the old inside forward role. I was the one doing all the work. It was very difficult to score goals there."

This was the case even though Torino's captain was midfielder Enzo Bearzot who, as an attack-minded manager, guided the Italian national side to World Cup glory in 1982. Joe put the style of play down to the bonuses. "Players have the choice between a risky policy of attack with up to £80 each if they win, or safe defensive play with £40 for a draw – many teams play for the smaller prize," he explained. The British duo's first league game for Torino was a 2-0 defeat away to Sampdoria on 27 August, but both got off the mark the following week during an uncharacteristically Italian 3-3 draw at home to Lanerossi Vicenza (now Vicenza Calcio). Joe put the ball on a plate for Law to put Torino ahead early on. Two goals from Joe – the second from a virtually impossible angle – gave them a 3-1 half-time lead but, after the break, he realised that successfully unlocking the door-bolt could come at a price.

"Play had stopped because a player was injured," he recalled. "For no reason at all, one of the opposing players ran up to me and tried to poke his fingers into my eyes. He could have blinded me. I was so angry I took a kick at him. Then the referee stepped in, and of course it was me who was sent off." With Italian league matches played on Sundays, Gerry, who had made the trip to watch Joe's home debut, says: "After the game, he came up to me and said: 'You can tell Mum I'll be home this week!'"

In 118 matches during four seasons at Hibs, Joe had never been sent off and, here he was, getting his marching orders during his very first home game for Torino. His scoring record read two games, two goals, but he was fined and received a one-match suspension. The sense of injustice made Joe bitter and, almost immediately, he was beginning to regret his big move.

"The Italians play the dirtiest football I've ever seen," he complained at the time, later adding: "I found life in Italy great but the football was ter-rible, brutal. There was spitting, kicking, elbowing, things I was never used to, although I didn't mind playing hard. You could have the ball anywhere in your own half, but, as soon as you came within 30 yards of the opposition's goal, they put you in a coffin. The defenders were suicide men. You soon learned that the best policy was to stay yards away from the nearest defender, otherwise you were given an elbow in the face, had the hairs in the back of your legs pulled out, or took a dig in the kidneys."

Joe also admitted that having a poor grasp of the language had its advantages. "The crowds here go crazy during a match and it is probably just as well we don't hear what they're calling us when they're shaking the barbed-wire fence," he said.

Eighty miles away, in Milan, Joe's England team-mate Jimmy Greaves was finding life in Italy equally intolerable. One of the game's greatest ever finishers hated the defensive tactics. He also hated the curfews, his employers and just about everything else the country had to offer. Greaves agreed with Joe's view that, "When an Italian club buys a player they really think they own him body and soul." And although he didn't stick around in Italy long enough to face Torino, Greaves did bump into Joe and Law on a rail journey south, where the three unhappy Brits abroad took time to air their grievances.

"I remember Joe and I meeting Jimmy on the train," explains Law. "We'd heard that he wasn't very happy and he told us that he was desperate to get back home. He didn't stay in Italy long. He wouldn't have been there much longer than three months but he was a fantastic player and he was still the third highest goalscorer for Milan at the end of that season. For me and Joe, it had just become a matter of playing out a bit of time before we could get back to Britain as well."

Law's assertion that whoever scored first usually won is borne out by the fact that three of Joe's seven league goals that season came in 1-0 victories. And none of these went down better than the one he scored on 1 October at the Stadio Comunale. Although Torino's main home was the Stadio Filadelfia, the Comunale was where they played their biggest home matches, against the likes of Milan and Internazionale. It was also the home of their greatest rivals, the team from whom their dissident club had formed: Juventus. "When you talk about British derby games like Rangers and Celtic, Hibs and Hearts, United and City, Liverpool and Everton, Arsenal and Spurs, they had nothing on Juventus and Torino," says Law. "This was war. When Joe scored the winner, we felt like kings. After the game, we were driving back on the team coach and we saw Torino supporters marching a fake coffin, draped in the colours of Juventus, through the city centre. That was a huge game for us, especially as the great John Charles was on the other side."

Law and Joe made a brief return to Britain with Torino in the autumn to play friendlies against their respective former clubs. First up was Gerry's Manchester City in a midweek game at Maine Road on 11 October. Although City won 4-3, with Gerry getting the fourth, Joe scored a hat-trick. "I couldn't believe it when I saw Joe at Maine Road," recalls Gerry. "He was built like a bull. He looked like he'd been training with Arnold Schwarzenegger. He was so muscular that his legs could barely get into his shorts – he must've been filling up with spaghetti!" That weekend, an understrength Torino, although featuring both British players, lost 2-0 in a disappointing match at Easter Road.

For Joe, the match against City was a reminder of how much more freedom was to be had in British football. He and Law were only back in Italy for a few weeks before they travelled to Glasgow for a challenge match between the Scottish League and the Italian League. The four British players in the Italian squad: Joe, Law, Charles and Hitchens, were pictured training together near Hampden Park, the word "Italia" emblazoned across their tracksuits. But when it came to the starting XI being announced, only the latter three expats were on the Italian team sheet. Joe immediately stormed out of the Italian League's hotel and made straight for Motherwell, defying strict orders that the British players were not to visit their homes. "I had my heart set on playing at Hampden," he fumed. "Why did they bring me to Scotland if they were not going to play me in a match being played only 20 minutes from my home? It's a terrible disappointment."

Law, who was sharing a room with Joe at the hotel, said: "I knew Joe was disappointed, but was surprised when I went into our room and found his bag gone. Joe knows that discipline is strict in Italian football. I hope he doesn't do anything silly." Joe re-joined the Italian party later that night, after they had secured a 1-1 draw. Joe's mood didn't improve when he was also left out of the side that drew with the English Football League at Old Trafford a week later.

But for all Joe's disappointment at not being picked for the League representative matches, his goal return on Italian soil had not gone unnoticed by the Torino supporters. By the time Sampdoria visited the Filadelfia on Christmas Eve, 1961, he had found the net six times – no mean feat in a league with the lowest goal average in world football. With an hour gone and the match goalless, Joe was scythed down. "It was a vicious tackle," he said. "He took a wild swing at me. If it had landed properly I would have hit the moon."

Again Joe retaliated, and again the referee pointed to the changing rooms. With, according to one newspaper report, "tears in his eyes", Joe was cheered from the field by the home support. "Joe was a fiery character – both of us were," admits Law. "If people are constantly kicking you, you're not just going to say, 'That's okay, you keep kicking me.' You'd retaliate and of course you'd get sent off."

Joe's tears may have had more to do with the fact that he was losing his wages even quicker than he was losing his temper. Even for a player earning £100 a week, a fine of £225 was hard to stomach. "This fine is automatic under the rules of the Italian League," explained club secretary Gino Guisti. "This is the second ordering off and two-game suspension Joe has had since he joined us, and we cannot afford to have the same thing happen again."

Joe, however, felt he was being victimised. "A British player abroad is a marked man – on and off the field," he claimed. "He must be good – otherwise a foreign club wouldn't have paid an enormous fee for him. His transfer is given tremendous publicity. The other clubs are ready and waiting for him. One man in each team is given the job of marking him for the match. It's like having a constant shadow." Law, naturally, came in for similar treatment, but had so far managed to avoid being given his marching orders. The Scotsman was more reluctant to retaliate, mainly because: "I was a little wimp compared to Joe. I was just a piece of flesh and bone, whereas he was really tough and strong."

The latest suspension meant that Joe would be ineligible to play until Torino's visit to Venezia on 14 January. This time, the man quickly gaining a reputation as one of the bad boys of Italian football didn't even make it as far as the field before trouble came calling. A stroll by Venice's Grand Canal would normally be considered a relaxing pastime but, for Joe and Law, their walk was anything but peaceful. While the pair were unprepared for the tight defences and strict discipline of life in Italy, they were equally unprepared for the close attentions of the paparazzi. Exactly what happened between Joe and photographer Celio Scapin by the side of the canal has become the stuff of legend. Although it is tempting to believe the tales of Joe picking up the snapper and hurling him head-first into the water, the player later revealed this was merely wishful thinking. "Whenever Denis and I got into bother in Italy he'd give as good as he got with his tongue," he said. "But I'm no great talker. In really bad trouble I prefer to use my fists."

Law says: "We were walking alongside the canal and there were two photographers snapping away. We were telling them, 'You've taken your photographs, now off you go.' But (Scapin) kept taking the photographs so Joe, with his fiery temper, gave him a bit of a batter. Well, it was just one punch really." But one punch was all it took for Joe to land himself with yet another suspension, with Torino themselves deciding that he wouldn't play against Venice for fear of inciting trouble among the crowd. "It would have been a nightmare if he'd played," admits Law. "I think he'd have been lynched if he'd been on the pitch."

To make matters worse, Torino fined Joe for not turning out. "If I'd thought it was going to cost me all that I would really have had my money's worth and thrown him into the Grand Canal as well," he said. Joe scored in his second game back, a 2-1 defeat in Bologna, but then a 3-1 win for Juventus saw him unable to repeat the heroics of his first Turin derby. The match, played on 4 February, turned out to be Joe's last appearance in a Torino jersey for more than two months. He was lucky it wasn't his last appearance anywhere.

Gerry, who by now was doing his best to fill the void left by his brother at Easter Road, was on his way to train with Hibs when he heard the news on the radio. He pulled over at the nearest telephone kiosk to ring his mother. Joe had been involved in a car accident, he explained. He didn't know how badly he was hurt, but he was to undergo emergency surgery in a Turin hospital. The family would have to fly out immediately.

The drama had begun to unfold the previous day, when Joe had taken delivery of his new sports car – a white Alfa Romeo Giulietta Sprint. At £2,000, it was a symbol of the superstar football lifestyle, a considerable step up from Joe's Fiat 500. From the get-go, the signs were ominous. "It was so fast I almost knocked down the salesman as I took it from the garage," he said afterwards.

With Law's brother Joseph over to visit, the trio had gone out for dinner with Gigi Peronace. Joe, Law and Joseph then returned to their apartment before heading to a nightclub. At around 4 am on 8 February, the trio got back in the car. John Foot describes what happened next in his book *Calcio: A History of Italian Football*:

Baker was at the wheel, with Denis Law next to him and Joseph behind. Driving at relatively high speed . . . Baker attempted to take a corner without slowing down adequately. His car caught the edge of a wall below one of Turin's monuments to Italian hero Giuseppe Garibaldi (the papers joked that Baker had failed to 'dribble past Garibaldi'). The vehicle then flipped onto its back, spun again and crashed into a lamppost thirty metres down the road. Baker smashed his head against the steering wheel, breaking his palate, his nose, both his cheekbones and his jaw. His face was covered in bits of glass.

Law was more or less unhurt and Law's brother escaped without a scratch.

Joe's mother, stepfather Davie and girlfriend Sonia had already planned to come to Italy to watch Joe play against Udinese that weekend. What should have been Sonia's first football match in Italy turned into a bedside vigil, but not before the paparazzi had descended on the San Giovanni Hospital. "I had plastic surgery immediately," said Joe later. "They took the skin off my hand. What I couldn't get over was that half an hour after the crash they allowed the photographers into the operating theatre. It was absolutely ridiculous. The surgeons let them in to take photographs of me lying struggling on the table, blood dripping all ways. Some of the pictures were horrific."

But the intrusion didn't end there. After several weeks of injections, drinking food through a straw and "tearing at the bedclothes in pain", the police paid Joe a visit, seeking assurances that his £2,300 hospital bills would be paid. Then came the wrath of Peronace. "I trusted them too much," he snapped. "Maybe the bright lights of this city were too big a temptation. I told Joe not to buy that £2,000 sports car. It wasn't for a footballer. But Joe was *crazy*, wouldn't listen – and he's paid a high price. I hope they have learned their lesson."

Torino, whose insurance paid for Joe's treatment, cracked down hard, not least because reports of a 4 am car crash meant the players had broken their strict 10 pm curfew. Law, nursing little more than a cut hand, was suspended for the next match and fined £320. Joe's contract was cut until the end of the season (due to the World Cup, the last league fixture had been brought forward to 15 April), meaning he forfeited all wages and bonuses during his two months in hospital.

Speaking, with difficulty, from his hospital bed, Joe said: "I'm all for the quiet life and you just can't get that here. I've been in Italy for eight months and every month I am in the headlines over something or other. I don't like it. I know now what Jimmy Greaves went through and I only hope that if Torino do transfer me it won't be a long drawn-out affair as it was with Jimmy. I have read that they are thinking of transferring me. If that is the case I can only say I would jump at the chance to get back home."

Still hoping that a British club would come to his rescue, Joe made his comeback for Torino on 25 April, in the 2-0 Coppa Italia quarter-final defeat at home to Serie B side Napoli. Joe was given an opportunity to score just before half-time when Torino were awarded a penalty. Although not a regular spot-kick taker, the home fans, delighted to see the return of their

English hero, cried out for Joe to take it. Understandably out of touch, Joe's side-footed effort presented Pacifico Cuman with a comfortable save, but the main talking point of the match came just after the break.

Having already been refused permission to play for Scotland in an upcoming friendly against Uruguay, Law was sent off – at the behest of his own coach, Beniamino Santos, who felt that the Scot, particularly with Joe having just returned to the side, was spending too much time in his own half. Santos called over the Torino skipper, Enzo Bearzot, and ordered him to ask the referee for Law's expulsion. Angry, and understandably bemused, Law left the field in Italy for the last time. Although still desperate for a move, Joe was touched by the fact the home fans shouted his name at the final whistle.

After a massive bust-up with the Torino president following his dismissal, Law was banned from the ground for two weeks, but travelled with Joe and the rest of the squad to Lausanne at the beginning of May for the opening game of the Italian-French-Swiss Cup of Friendship, a 16-team tournament played across all three nations. It was while in Switzerland for the first leg against Lausanne-Sport that Law met up with Matt Busby to discuss a possible transfer to Manchester United. It was also where Joe began to rediscover his form.

After playing in the 2-1 victory in Switzerland, he opened the scoring in the return leg in Turin after only two minutes, with another 2-1 win securing Torino's place in the quarter-finals against Lyon. In the first leg in France, Joe again opened the scoring, this time after 14 minutes, in yet another 2-1 win. It was a signal to any potentially interested British clubs that Joe's footballing ability had not suffered as a result of his accident.

A few weeks after his initial meeting with Busby, Law walked out on Torino, saying he was tired of being treated like "a side of beef". He left the apartment, leaving a note for Joe, and, on 10 July, was bought for £115,000 by Manchester United, the club where he would forge his legend. His friend's transfer left Joe a fiver out of pocket, after the pair had bet on who would be the first to secure a move back to a British club. Joe admitted that, without Law's friendship in Italy, he'd have "gone crazy". With two matches of the Cup of Friendship remaining, he was effectively on his own and, with Torino dragging their heels over whether they should let a second star player go, it called for drastic measures. "I had to go to Italy and kidnap him," explains Gerry. "He couldn't escape. I was there for a week trying to get him out. In the end, we had to take as much as we could from the apartment in one go. I was wearing four overcoats and a hat in 90-degree heat – I nearly melted at the airport, but it helped disguise us from the photographers."

From the safety of his mum's home in Motherwell, a world away from his luxury apartment in Turin, Joe told reporters that he was finished with Italian football and, reluctantly, Torino agreed that they would be willing to sell him. Joe ruled out a return to a Scottish club, believing that joining an English team would boost his chances of regaining his place in the national side. Gerry, meanwhile, had spent nearly the whole of the preceding season playing back in Scotland, and the task he had faced wasn't an enviable one.

13
Baker's Brother

Trying to replace a man who has scored more than a century of goals in under four seasons is a tall order for any striker; stepping into the boots of a player who has achieved god-like status among the support is daunting; but when that player is your little brother, the task is nigh on impossible.

Gerry Baker, who left Manchester City to take over as the new No.9 at Hibs in late 1961, shrugs and says, "It didn't bother me in the slightest."

The 23-year-old, and by now father of one, had become frustrated at Maine Road. Several spells in and out of the reserves towards the end of his first season had been a source of irritation and, although Gerry had enjoyed a promising start to his second campaign, by mid-September he was being asked to play on the wing, while new striker Peter Dobing was scoring goals for fun.

Looking back on the day he told manager Les McDowall that he'd had enough, Gerry admits his decision may have been hasty. "I was an idiot, a big mouth and I didn't have a brain in my head," he says. "Manchester City had been doing well in the league and I told him I was unhappy about being put in the reserves and then not being played at centre-forward. I told him I wanted to be transferred. Unfortunately, he took me at my word."

Gerry went public with his feelings on 11 November, announcing: "I have no complaints against Manchester City – but I want a move back to Scotland. I feel I am getting nowhere here."

His wish was granted less than a week later, by the club at which his brother had been such a success, and shortly after the end of an era at Easter Road. After a poor start to the season with only two wins in ten games, Hugh Shaw, the former Hibs player who had guided the club to three league championships since he took over in 1948, left the club on 6 November 1961. Under the interim management of chairman Harry Swan, who had let the younger Baker brother leave for the sake of an extra £5 a week, Hibs signed Gerry on 17 November, using £17,000 of Joe's transfer fee. One thing was for certain, Maine Road would be a quieter place from now on.

"If he'd been able to stay longer at the club, I think Gerry could have had a good career at Manchester City," says former Sky Blues winger Roy Cheetham. "He was a great goal-poacher, he was a great lad and he got on with everybody. I thought we had plenty of good players, but unfortunately we just didn't have a good team – it happens sometimes. Things at Manchester City only changed dramatically when Joe Mercer and Malcolm Allison came along in 1965. And then suddenly you had the feeling that everything was going to change for the better. There was a spark and confidence about the club and you could see they were going to move forward. But before that they were quite lean times."

And none leaner than in 1963, when City were relegated. Steve Fleet, Bert Trautmann's understudy at City, says Gerry was a "knapsack-on-my-back type of person" and, as he joined his fifth senior club at the age of 23, it would be difficult to argue.

Still, he was glad to be back home in Motherwell with his wife and baby daughter Karen and he was looking forward to playing for Hibs, whose famous forward line he and Joe had admired from the Fir Park terracing as children. Hibs' decision to replace brother with brother was not completely unheard of. There had been a similar situation in Glasgow five years earlier, when Billy McPhail stepped into his older sibling John's shooting boots as centre-forward at Celtic. Although he was at Parkhead for only two seasons, Billy did enough to write himself into Hoops folklore when he scored a hat-trick in a 7-1 win over Rangers.

Gerry would, of course, have to go some way to replace Joe in the affections of Hibs supporters, something he was doubtless reminded of during one of his last games for City, when Joe scored a hat-trick for Torino.

"Gerry had a lot of the gifts his brother had," says veteran Edinburgh journalist John Gibson, "but who, in all honesty, could be up to Joe Baker's mark?"

Gerry missed out on the opportunity to make his European debut by a matter of days, with Hibs losing 5-0 on aggregate to Red Star Belgrade in the second round of the Fairs Cup. With Hibs second bottom of the First Division, Gerry made his bow in the league at St Johnstone. He didn't score, but goals from Eric Stevenson and John Fraser gave Hibs only their third league win of the season.

"Gerry was some character," recalls Fraser, who also played alongside Joe throughout his four seasons at the club. "I remember him bringing a big flash American car into training. He had a label from a beer bottle on the dashboard. When I asked him what it was for, he said it was his road tax! On the pitch, he had wonderful pace. We thought Joe was fast, but his brother was even faster. He also scored plenty of goals."

The first of which could hardly have been more fitting. Losing 2-0 at Love Street against St Mirren at the beginning of December, Hibs scored three times in the space of 15 second-half minutes, with Gerry scoring the winner against his old club.

It was Gerry's third game since his return to Scottish football and his second under manager Walter Galbraith, who had been given the job at Easter Road despite overseeing Tranmere Rovers' relegation to the English Fourth Division the previous season. The Hibs board initially wanted to appoint Dunfermline manager Jock Stein, but the Fife club refused to let him go – at least for now.

Next up for Hibs was a competition in which Gerry had consistently proven his goalscoring ability – the Scottish Cup. And he lived up to his reputation when he scored twice away to Partick Thistle to put Hibs within two minutes of the second round. Leading 2-1, Hibs threw everyone bar Gerry into defence for the last 15 minutes, and there was a certain in-evitability about Partick's late equaliser from a corner. The Glasgow side went one better in the replay, beating Hibs 3-2 at Easter Road. Partick also finished above Hibs in the league, with Galbraith's side eighth come the end of the season.

"We didn't set the Scottish world alight," admitted Gerry at the time, "but I felt that we came through a sticky patch well enough to give us heart and hope for the new season. I have roved quite a bit in my brief football career, but there is something you cannot quite put into words about play-ing with and before your own folk. Yet I don't think I am any the worse for the varied experience I have had."

After scoring 12 goals in 23 games in his first season, Gerry joined his new team-mates, including future Scotland manager Ally MacLeod, on a post-season tour of Czechoslovakia. The trip behind the Iron Curtain proved to be an eye-opening experience for Gerry. "I had never seen tanks on street corners before," he says. "We went on a tour around Prague and I remember seeing people queuing. Our guide warned us not to stare. He told us the people were queuing for food because they were starving."

Hibs coach Eddie Turnbull warned the players not to be picky about the food they were served at their hotel, but Gerry's caution was vindicated. "I was handed a plate with a tattie that had horns on it," he says. "I said, 'Er, I'll just have the soup.' Eddie Turnbull said, 'Just fucking eat it.' I didn't, and neither did any of the other players. Eddie did . . . and he spent the rest of the tour in bed with food poisoning."

A fit and healthy Gerry performed well during the tour, and his two goals in Ostrava seemed to be putting Hibs on course for a straightforward win against FC Vitkovice. But as part of a city sports festival that had already seen the televised match held up for the arrival of parachutists into the stadium, it was then abandoned altogether to allow workers to erect a stand for a bicycle race. "I've seen matches abandoned due to bad weather and floodlight failure, but I'd never seen one abandoned because of a bike race," laughs Gerry.

With such a scenario unlikely in Scotland, Gerry began his first full season at Hibs with goals against two of his former clubs: in a 3-3 draw with St Mirren in the League Cup and in a 2-2 draw with Motherwell in the league. In the former competition, he also registered his first Hibs hat-trick in a 4-1 win over Third Lanark – a club against whom Joe had regularly shown a particular aptitude for scoring.

After consecutive league hidings against Rangers and Dundee United, Gerry marked his first appearance in a European game with a goal in an easy 4-0 win over Danish part-timers Staevnet at Easter Road. He scored again in the narrow second-round victory over Utrecht but, not for the first time, Hibs' European adventure ended in emphatic defeat. In the first leg of their quarter-final in Spain, they were trounced 5-0 by Valencia. When Gerry's spectacular header put Hibs 2-0 up after only 24 minutes in the second leg at Easter Road, it seemed an unlikely comeback might be on, but the Spaniards held firm for the rest of the match, with the eventual winners safely progressing into the last four.

Although the 2-1 win over Valencia on 3 April was ultimately in vain, the way Hibs had played belied their league position – deep in relegation trouble with only three wins from 22 matches. The European victory had a galvanising effect on the club, and on Gerry in particular. After losing 2-0 at Celtic, Gerry scored six times in four consecutive league matches, including a hat-trick in the 3-1 win over Dundee.

Heading into the final three games of the campaign, Hibs were still in the relegation zone. To give themselves the best possible chance of staying up, they would need to do what they hadn't done all season – win three matches on the bounce.

When they went 1-0 down to St Mirren after only ten minutes, the meagre Easter Road crowd of 4,000 had their doubts, only for John Baxter to equalise on the hour and for Gerry to grab the winner shortly afterwards. He scored twice more in a 4-0 win over Queen of the South and again in another 4-0 win away to bottom club Raith Rovers. Hibs, thanks in no small part to Gerry's 13 goals in 23 league games, had survived by the skin of their teeth.

Although it was clear that, entering the 1963-64 season, Walter Galbraith's coat was on a particularly shoogly peg, he made another astute signing during the close season, bringing in the free-scoring Neil Martin

The young Gerry, left, and Joe with their parents Lizzie and George outside their home in Wishaw, circa 1947.

Joe and Gerry in 1952. "We were like twins," says Gerry.

Joe, second from right in the front row, poses for a trophy-winning photograph with the rest of the Park Street Primary football team in Motherwell in 1953.

Joe, far right in the back row, lines up with Scotland Schoolboys ahead of his debut against Wales at Somerset Park, Ayr, on 7 May 1955. Future Liverpool stalwart Willie Stevenson is far left in the same row, while Sammy Reid, Bill Shankly's first signing at Anfield, is second from left in the middle row.

Gerry, right, wearing his Chelsea blazer, gets ready to travel down to London with Joe in the summer of 1955.

Joe with Gordon Smith – an idol who became a team-mate. A member of Hibs' Famous Five, Smith was astounded by Joe's pace.

Gerry wheels away after chipping Aberdeen goalkeeper Dave Walker to put St Mirren 3-0 up in front of 108,000 spectators in the Scottish Cup final on 25 April 1959.

Playing at a snow-covered Love Street, Gerry scores one of his record-breaking ten goals as St Mirren begin their defence of the Scottish Cup with a 15-0 win over Glasgow University on 30 January 1960.

Clyde defenders protest as 17-year-old Joe puts the ball into the net with his hand during Hibs'
Scottish Cup final defeat of 1958. (*The Scotsman Publications Ltd*)

Hibernian's Joe and St Mirren's Gerry meet for the first time in their professional careers in a Scottish First Division match at Love Street on 22 November 1958. Gerry scored the decisive goal in a
2-1 win for St Mirren.

Joe Baker, the teenager from Motherwell, tries his new England shirt on for size ahead of his senior international debut in November 1959.

He may have had a Scottish accent, but Joe's commitment to England was never in doubt, as he demonstrates in this picture taken during their defeat to Hungary in Budapest on 22 May 1960.

Joe Baker (left) and Denis Law in the land of sunshine and Soccer fortunes.

FANS ARE NOT SO FIERCE AS THE SCOTS

A slightly misleading headline in *Charles Buchan's Football Monthly* accompanies a picture of Joe Baker and Denis Law turning out for Torino in 1961. (*Football Monthly Ltd*)

The Italian League's all-star line-up of British players: Gerry Hitchens (Internazionale), John Charles (Juventus), Denis Law (Torino) and Joe Baker (Torino) train outside Hampden Park ahead of their meeting with the Scottish League in November 1961. Joe was furious when he found out he had not been selected for the match. (*The Scotsman Publications Ltd*)

Joe demonstrates his skills for youngsters in Turin during his single season in Italy in 1961-62.

Joe, Denis Law and Joseph Law were lucky to escape with their lives following a crash in Joe's Alfa Romeo Giulietta Sprint in Turin in February 1962. Joe suffered serious facial injuries and spent several weeks in hospital. (*Topfoto*)

Gerry meets up with former team-mate Denis Law and brother Joe ahead of Manchester City's friendly with Torino in 1961. (*Mirrorpix*)

Gerry picked up where his brother left off by scoring in the colours of Hibs, this time against St Johnstone at Easter Road. (*The Scotsman Publications Ltd*)

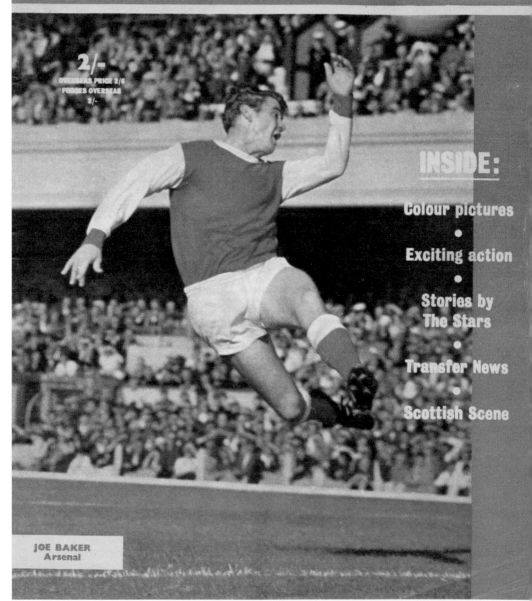

CHARLES BUCHAN'S

FOOTBALL
MONTHLY

APRIL, 1965

The
World's
Greatest
Soccer
Magazine

2/-
OVERSEAS PRICE 2/6
FORCES OVERSEAS
2/-

INSIDE:

Colour pictures

Exciting action

Stories by
The Stars

Transfer News

Scottish Scene

JOE BAKER
Arsenal

Joe, who scored a century of goals for Arsenal in just three and a half seasons at Highbury, appears on the front cover of *Charles Buchan's Football Monthly* in April 1965. (*Football Monthly Ltd*)

Joe, front row, centre, lines up with some very familiar faces while training with England on 1 January 1966. Back row, from left: Gordon Banks, Tony Walters, Jack Charlton, Bobby Moore, George Cohen, Ray Wilson. Front row, from left: Roger Hunt, Bobby Charlton, Joe Baker, John Connelly, Nobby Stiles. The 1-1 draw with Poland four days later marked Joe's last appearance in an England shirt. (*Getty Images*)

New England manager Alf Ramsey addresses his squad, including Joe Baker (centre of picture), ahead of the European Cup of Nations qualifier against France in February 1963. It was the first time in three years that Joe had been included in the senior squad, but he would have to wait until 1965 before he played for England again. (*Mirrorpix*)

England's new striker Joe Baker faces the cameras ahead of his debut against Northern Ireland at Wembley on 18 November 1959. (*The Scotsman Publications Ltd*)

Goalkeeper Jose Angel Iribar is beaten by Joe's close-range shot only eight minutes into England's friendly against Spain at the Bernabeu on 8 December 1965. Alf Ramsey later admitted that it was after this 2-0 win that he firmly believed his side could win the World Cup, but Joe limped off after half an hour and played just one more game for the national side. (*Topfoto*)

Joe's story-so-far is presented in comic strip form in *Charles Buchan's Football Monthly* in November 1967. (*Football Monthly Ltd*)

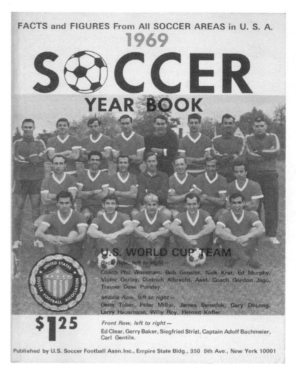

In stark contrast to his brother, Gerry Baker had to wait until the twilight of his career before he got his first taste of international football, becoming the first top-flight European player to represent the United States when he made his debut against Canada in October 1968. He is pictured, front row, second from left, with the rest of the American squad on the front cover of the 1969 *Soccer Year Book*. (*Courtesy of Jim Trecker and the United States Soccer Federation*)

Gerry, standing in the centre of the picture wearing his United States blazer, joins the rest of his American colleagues, including coach Phil Woosnam (checked suit) at Francois 'Papa Doc' Duvalier's palace in Haiti in October 1968. Note the dictator's portrait on the rear wall.

The crowd at Easter Road trebled to see Joe Baker – complete with white boots and sideburns – make his second debut for Hibs on 16 January 1971, nearly ten years after he had left the club to join Torino. He gave his fans what they wanted by scoring in a 2-1 win over Eddie Turnbull's Aberdeen. (*The Scotsman Publications Ltd*)

Joe signs autographs for star-struck young Hibs fans during his Easter Road heyday. (*The Scotsman Publications Ltd*)

Gerry, left, and Joe compare their respective Scottish Cup winner and runner-up trophies at home in Wishaw in 1959. Sadly, silverware would elude Joe throughout his career. (*The Scotsman Publications Ltd*)

Joe proudly displays his England, and Scotland Schoolboy, caps at home with son Colin and wife Sonia in 1983. (*The Scotsman Publications Ltd*)

from Queen of the South. Martin, who would later play alongside Gerry at Coventry City, immediately justified his £7,500 transfer fee, as six goals from him, and seven from Gerry, helped Hibs reach the semi-finals of the League Cup – their best performance in the competition for a decade.

Then, two days before their semi-final showdown with Greenock Morton at Ibrox, Galbraith introduced a youngster to the side who would go on to become one of the club's all-time greats. Pat Stanton, then aged 19, had been in the Hibs ranks for a year before scoring on his debut, alongside Gerry and Martin in the 4-3 defeat to Motherwell on 5 October 1963.

"Gerry was a real bundle of laughs and he was a big help to me in terms of advice," says Stanton. "On the field, like his brother, he was very quick, very strong and very determined. He obviously knew what a hero Joe had been to the Hibs fans and, when you were talking to Gerry about him, you could see that he was very proud of Joe. Both Gerry and Joe would smile away off the park but, once they were on it, they had an insatiable appetite to win."

But Stanton and Gerry would play together only on another four occasions before Gerry decided that he had had enough. After a 1-1 draw in the first match at Ibrox, Hibs were beaten by Morton in the League Cup semi-final replay. Come March, Walter Galbraith would resign and be replaced by Jock Stein. But by the time the future European Cup winner arrived at Easter Road, Gerry had already returned to English football, playing for a club that showed what can happen when the top job goes to the wrong man.

14
Tractor Boy

A great footballer does not necessarily make a great manager. If that isn't a well-worn football mantra, then perhaps it should be. A list of outstanding players who were unable to cut the managerial mustard, including the likes of Alan Ball, Bryan Robson and Bobby Charlton, would be enough to fill a book.

Meanwhile, some of the game's most successful managers – Bill Shankly, Alex Ferguson and Jock Stein – while decent players, hardly set the turf alight. Whether being Scottish makes one innately predisposed to managerial proficiency is perhaps another matter entirely. Unfortunately for fans of Ipswich Town, Jackie Milburn, the Geordie hero who, like Joe Baker, saw his supreme striking talent criminally underused by England, fell firmly into the former category.

Indeed, even Robson, with three relegations at three different clubs, would have had trouble emulating the spectacular demise of Ipswich Town under Milburn. Nor would Charlton, the World Cup winner whose brief tenure at Preston North End is still talked about for all the wrong reasons, be quick to swap his managerial record with his mother's Uncle Jackie.

It's true that Milburn's predecessor gave him a lot to live up to. In 1962, after seven years at the helm, Alf Ramsey guided the Suffolk club to their first – and, to date, only – league championship. Leading what appeared to be an ordinary side that had been tipped by many for relegation to the summit of the English game was a feat so remarkable that, five months later, he was named manager of the national side – the ultimate result of which was enough to keep England fans fruitlessly dreaming of further success for many years to come.

The future Sir Alf's England contract would not begin until April 1963, which would leave plenty of time for cracks to appear at Portman Road. The main problem, pointed out by Ramsey's biographer Leo McKinstry, was that, aside from a general lack of interest in scouting and reserve players, the manager possessed an "almost reckless loyalty". Apart from buying Bobby Blackwood from Hearts, Ramsey's squad for the 1962-63 season was exactly the same as the one that won him the championship. And with several members of the squad having peaked during that unforgettable campaign, signs of fatigue were beginning to show. "We struggled because we were stuck with what we had," explained former Ipswich star Ray Crawford.

After a far-from-convincing season that included a number of heavy defeats, the league champions' top-flight status was already under serious threat when Milburn, a former England team-mate of Ramsey's, arrived on the scene in January 1963.

"Wor Jackie", who had beaten 60 other applicants to the post, was under the impression that Ramsey would be at Ipswich only until April, and then only in an advisory capacity. But, with Ramsey apparently carrying on a grudge from their playing days and refusing to relinquish control, Milburn was given the cold-shoulder treatment, even being excluded from team-talks.

"That couldn't have been very nice for Jackie," admits championship winner Doug Moran. "It couldn't have done his confidence much good." Milburn officially took charge of Ipswich with four league games remaining, with two draws and two defeats enough to see the Tractor Boys stave off relegation by four points. Narrowly avoiding the drop was as good as it was going to get for Milburn.

"From the moment he arrived, it was clear he did not have much idea about what was going on," said defender Andy Nelson. "Alf refused to leave until the club was safe and he was right, because within 12 months Jackie had devastated the place. He was absolutely clueless."

The following season started promisingly with a 3-1 win at home to Burnley but, by the time Gerry Baker arrived in December, this was still the only victory Ipswich had managed to rack up in 20 league games. It wasn't just the number of defeats that was alarming to Ipswich supporters, however, but rather the kamikaze manner in which they went about them. The team's losses were nothing if not spectacular. On nine occasions during the season, they shipped six goals or more.

Their second home game saw Denis Law score a hat-trick in a 7-2 defeat to Manchester United, whom Ipswich had actually finished above during the previous campaign. A month later, following a 6-0 cuffing at Bolton, Joe Baker got in on the act, helping himself to a brace as they lost 6-0 at Arsenal.

The problems didn't lie solely in defence. During the 20 matches prior to Gerry's arrival, Ipswich had managed to muster only 19 goals. It was clear that, as well as an industrial-sized plug at the back, Milburn was in desperate need of some extra firepower up front – particularly as he had decided to sell the prolific Ray Crawford to Wolves for £50,000 in September.

While his record for Hibs wasn't quite as impressive as his brother's, Gerry's total of 43 goals in 83 games meant that he was still a sought-after striker. Although not, perhaps, as sought after as he was led to believe. "I wasn't really given a choice when it came to signing for Ipswich," he says. "Eddie Turnbull, who was an influential coach at Hibs, was a great guy but if you crossed him you were out the door. That's just the way he was. Joe never got on with him either. I had been playing well and there were rumours in the newspapers that I was going to sign for Celtic. I don't know where the story came from but I think I was maybe starting to believe my own publicity. I was a bit cocky and asked Eddie what he thought about me getting a wee rise. I thought, 'Well, there's no-one else scoring' and I was only getting about 40 quid a week, so I pushed my luck.

"Eddie sent me to see the chairman, Harry Swan, who said, 'I hear you're asking for an extra fiver? Don't you be reading the newspapers saying Celtic are doing this and Celtic are doing that. Celtic don't fucking want you.' He said, 'You're signing for Ipswich tomorrow.' Fine, I thought. But, to be honest, I didn't know quite how bad things were at Ipswich."

Gerry joined the Tractor Boys, now rock-bottom of the English First Division, for £17,000 in December 1963 – turning up in Suffolk just in time to see things go from bad to worse. His Portman Road career got off to a decent start, comparatively speaking – with a 0-0 draw against Blackburn. Gerry scored his first goal for Ipswich in the next game – a 3-1 defeat at Burnley. Then, just before Christmas, Ipswich fans saw something of a minor miracle. Their team enjoyed their first victory since the opening day of the season, with Gerry scoring the decider in a 3-2 win over West Ham. But if Ipswich fans thought this result was going to be a turning point in their miserable season, all of their Christmas nightmares were about to come true at once. On a bizarre Boxing Day of fixtures that saw 66 goals in the First Division, Ipswich travelled to Craven Cottage and were thumped 10-1 by Fulham. Scotland winger Graham Leggat got four goals, including a four-minute hat-trick, with Bobby Robson also getting involved. The result is still one that sends chills down Gerry's spine, even if he did score what turned out to be the least consoling of consolation goals.

The score raised plenty of eyebrows, and a few smiles at West Ham, if only because it detracted slightly from the fact that they had been beaten 8-2 by Blackburn.

"Nobody could believe how badly we defended," says Gerry. "The fog was rolling in off the Thames and I could barely see the other end of the pitch. I kept hearing cheer after cheer from the crowd as Fulham scored one goal after another. I got about 11 kicks of the ball in that game – one goal and ten kick-offs. I can finally laugh about it now, just about, but that result in particular left Jackie Milburn heartbroken.

"I can't imagine any chairmen doing this today, especially after a result like that, but John Cobbold took us all out for Christmas dinner afterwards. We were sitting in the restaurant, all wearing paper hats and feeling miserable, and Mr Cobbold raised a glass and said, 'Bollocks to it, lads, there's always tomorrow.' Then he decided to show us his latest trick – whipping off the tablecloth. There was broken crockery everywhere. Jackie was upstairs, hiding in his room, and I can't say I blame him."

Retribution – of sorts – for what Milburn described as "a freak result" was swift, as Ipswich won the return match 4-2 at Portman Road just two days later. Even better was to come after the New Year, as Gerry scored his first hat-trick in English football in a 6-3 third round FA Cup tie win over Oldham. This marked Ipswich's first back-to-back competitive victories since September 1962.

Having "inherited a team that was over the top and going downhill fast", it was obvious that Milburn would need to make some changes, but Gerry believes the reason for Ipswich's transformation from relegation contenders to relegation certainties was that these weren't more gradual.

Before Gerry arrived on the scene of devastation, Milburn had already signed nine players whom he felt could revive Town's fortunes. Apparently on a one-man crusade to make Ipswich a corner of England that would be forever Scotland, seven of these players – Jim Thorburn, George Dougan, John Bolton, John Colrain, Danny Hegan (a Northern Ireland international born in Coatbridge), Joe Davin and Frank Treacy – hailed from north of the Border. Along with Billy Baxter, Bobby Blackwood, Jimmy Leadbetter and Doug Moran – the Scottish players signed by Ramsey – Gerry could be forgiven for thinking he was still playing his football in Edinburgh.

"You'd never seen so many Scots in one place in your life," says Gerry. "Jackie was from Newcastle and played with the likes of Bobby Mitchell and Jimmy Scoular, so he had an affinity with Scottish players. Ramsey obviously liked Scottish players too. Jimmy Leadbetter was skinny but if he banged into you in training, you felt like you'd been hit by a motorbike."

Doug Moran believes the influx of his fellow countrymen had a negative effect on the side. "Jackie Milburn had queer ideas," he says. "He got rid of me (in April 1964) and got rid of Ray Crawford. Neither of us wanted to leave. Ray was a hero at Ipswich and Milburn transferred him to Wolves. He brought a lot of Scotsmen down and that was part of his downfall. He went up there and bought the centre-half (John Bolton) and goalkeeper (Jim Thorburn) from Raith Rovers and they'd just been relegated after conceding more than 100 goals. Jackie swamped the place with Scots but there should've been a happy medium of two or three. You can't have about eight Scotsmen in the team."

Ipswich could, however, afford to have one American, and Gerry's goals justified Milburn's assertion that he was "the centre-forward we need". Regardless of anyone's nationality, his task of overhauling a former championship-winning side that was well and truly on the wane was an uphill struggle from the start.

"To be honest, we weren't good enough," says Gerry. "I met Alf Ramsey a couple of times on the train, as he still lived in Ipswich. I got on all right with him and he didn't wish Ipswich any harm, but he was supposed to be helping Jackie and I don't think he did. I felt some of the players weren't trying hard enough for Jackie and that's why he had to start bringing his own guys in. Some of the ones that were there were over the hill. When you've been with one manager for 10-15 years, it can be difficult to adapt when someone takes over and doesn't think you can cut it any more. The truth is, you're not good enough but you don't know it until someone points it out to you."

But even with Milburn's batch of new players, the bad results kept on coming. In March 1964, a 6-0 defeat at Anfield was followed by a 9-1 thrashing at Stoke. Milburn handed in his resignation, only for chairman John Cobbold to assure him that, even if Ipswich were relegated (something that now looked a cast-iron certainty), he still wanted the Geordie in charge.

Even Gerry's hat-trick at White Hart Lane wasn't enough to secure a victory, with Cliff Jones also scoring three goals to help Spurs win 6-3. Five days after this defeat, on 9 April 1964, Gerry's family became complete when Anne gave birth to Lorraine. Just over 20 years later, Lorraine would put her father through "the most nerve-wracking experience of my life" when she competed in the 1984 Olympic Games in Los Angeles, finishing fifth in the final of the 800 metres. Two years later, she won a bronze medal at the Commonwealth Games in Edinburgh and, also in 1986, became only the fourth British woman to run the 800m in under two minutes. Karen, too, was an accomplished athlete, winning gold medals in the International Youth Games of 1974 and 1976.

Speed, it would seem, was in the Baker genes and, back in April 1964, her father's electrifying pace had helped him to score eight league goals during the final few weeks of the season, including a final-day hat-trick in a 4-3 win over Blackpool. It was all in vain, however, as Ipswich were relegated after scoring 56 goals and conceding 121. But even with a defensive record that remains one of the worst in the history of the English top-flight, Milburn kept his job as Ipswich returned to life in the Second Division.

The last time the club had played at this level, they had gone up as champions. Milburn was hopeful that his side could do the same but, after only one point from the first four matches, he admitted that he was "completely done in and no longer able to stand the pressure". Initially believing that his manager had been sacked, Gerry and a number of other players, including captain Bill Baxter, threatened to quit.

"If Jackie Milburn is leaving, I want to leave too," said Gerry at the time. "It's a drastic decision to take, but that's the way I feel about it . . . He has been good to me and I will do everything I can to support him. I don't want to stay at Ipswich without him."

Milburn's son, Jack, wrote that: "Dad was very touched by the display of loyalty, even though it was not enough to make him want to stay."

After handing in his resignation, Milburn said: "I have not lost confidence in myself as a manager, but results must speak for themselves. The strain and worry of the past year has been enormous and my health is beginning to be affected."

Gerry, who was persuaded by the board to stay, sighs and adds: "I loved Jackie. He was my hero and I played my guts out for that man. If you give everything, and you tried your best, the Ipswich fans would forgive you, but some of the results we had were ridiculous."

Doug Moran, one of the players sold by Milburn, says: "Jackie was a really nice bloke but some people are made to be managers and some aren't. He was one of the worst managers I've ever had. He got on too well with people."

The same could not be said of his successor, the former England international Bill McGarry. "He was a bugger," says Gerry. "The strictest manager ever. I remember his first game in charge, after we had drawn at Crystal Palace. On the bus he said, 'At least six of you will be out the door next week. Bloody Scotchmen.' I said, 'Excuse me, boss, but I'm an American.' I won't tell you what he said, but he nearly blasted me out the window!"

While Gerry took the window, McGarry spent the next few seasons showing numerous players the door. The manager had only narrowly failed to lead Watford to promotion from Division Three the previous season and was determined to take Ipswich back to the top flight as soon as possible. The club finished the 1964-65 season in fifth place. Gerry weighed in with 16 league goals, including one in the 7-0 rout of Portsmouth, but McGarry, a bit like his predecessor, was committed to making wholesale changes. By the summer of 1965, nine players had left Portman Road.

However, far from making progress, the team slumped to a 15th-place finish the following season. Gerry scored 15 goals in all competitions in what was ultimately a disappointing 1965-66. McGarry did, however, make two significant signings in the second half of the season. February saw the arrival of teenage full-back Mick Mills, who would go on to captain Ipswich to FA and UEFA Cup glory under Bobby Robson, while March saw Town fans rejoice in the return of Ray Crawford from Wolves. The £30,000 signing immediately showed the supporters what they had been missing, scoring eight goals in the last 12 games of the season. But as the summer of 1966 approached, the English sporting public was not overly concerned with how Ipswich fared – they were far more interested in the World Cup. And, against all the odds, it looked like the younger brother of an Ipswich striker might just have a part to play.

15
Indefensible

Joe Baker sank deep into his favourite armchair back home in Wishaw and pondered his next move. Following a daring escape from his internment in the north of Italy in the summer of 1962, the Torino striker had just been asked whether he would prefer to join a Scottish club or an English club. Joe's answer was straightforward. He stretched out his legs and replied: "An English club, because it would give me a better chance of getting back my place in their international team." His former team-mate Denis Law, who had the luxury of being first-pick for Scotland no matter where he was playing, had already sealed a record £115,000 move to Manchester United, but Joe still wasn't sure how straightforward his next move would be.

The interview over, Joe closed the door and asked himself a question. After all his high-profile problems at Torino – the indiscipline, both on and off the field, the inability to settle, to say nothing of a car crash that very nearly killed him, would any English club really be prepared to take a risk on the Baker boy? He didn't have to wait long for an answer. In fact, there seemed every chance that, having spent a year as flatmates in the north of Italy, Joe and Denis would now be neighbours in the north of England.

Gerry had already stepped into Joe's boots at Easter Road, now it looked like Joe would be taking his brother's place at Manchester City. Immediately after his return to British soil, the Maine Road club began negotiations to bring Joe to English football. Gerry's former employers reportedly offered Torino £28,000 – plus the £42,000 the Italians still owed them for the sale of Law – to take his 21-year-old brother to Manchester.

Perhaps understandably, Torino instead decided to accept the £70,000 cash offer tabled by Arsenal. The London club's trophy cabinet had been looking decidedly sparse in recent years. While their great rivals Tottenham had become the first English side to do the double in 1961, retaining the FA Cup the following season, Arsenal hadn't won the First Division championship for ten years. The only piece of silverware they had collected since then was the Southern Professional Floodlit Cup of 1959, something that still left them in the shadow of their North London neighbours. Frustrated by this lack of success, in early 1962 the Arsenal board elected to dismiss manager George Swindin, a former goalkeeper at Highbury, and replace him with Billy Wright.

Although his managerial experience was limited to the England youth team, Wright's credentials as a footballer were hard to match. At the time of his appointment in May 1962, the former England captain held the world record – 105 – for international appearances. Wright was a leader who commanded respect. His remit at Arsenal was simple: win trophies, win lots of them and, if it's at the expense of Tottenham, so much the better.

Wright had first encountered Joe at Easter Road during the twilight of his glittering career with Wolves. Although the Midlands club had won their 1957 friendly against Hibs, Wright had had to use all his football experience, with which he had defended against some of the greatest players in the world, to keep the 17-year-old at bay. The fact Wright had first recommended Joe to England manager Walter Winterbottom was further indication of how much he admired the striker.

But before spending a club record amount to bring Joe to England, Arsenal had to confirm there were no lingering effects from his Turin car crash. Before signing on the dotted line in the presence of Wright and agent Gigi Peronace in a Marble Arch hotel, Joe underwent more than two and a half hours' of extensive medical tests before he was declared "fully recovered". By this stage, he had already had several operations on his face and mouth, but decided to permanently delay what he called the "woman's operation" to straighten his nose. "He was on his way to the hospital but, after everything he had been through with the crash, he couldn't face more surgery," explains Gerry.

"We had to be sure, 100 per cent sure," said Wright. "We were paying a lot of money and we couldn't take chances." Joe signed for his first English club on 16 July 1962, the day before his 22nd birthday. "This is the happiest thing that has happened to me in football," he said. "I'm an Arsenal player at last. I've got a job to do for the greatest club in the country and I hope to do it well."

Joe spotted a couple of familiar faces at Highbury – his England Under-23 team-mate George Eastham, the player who had taken his previous employers, Newcastle United, to court in order to win his transfer, and Johnny MacLeod, whom he had played alongside at Armadale Thistle and then Hibs. The winger's departure from Easter Road had come just a few weeks after Joe had left for Torino. While Joe had asked for an extra fiver, MacLeod had paid the price for requesting another £2.

"Hibs didn't need the money, and what did they use it on?" he said. "They put another four railway sleepers up the top of the terracing, which were called Baker's Heights', with four urinals called 'MacLeod's lavvies'. They didn't buy anybody. To me it was such a waste selling Joe and me." Unlike the Hibs board, MacLeod appreciated his friend's value as a player. He said: "When Billy Wright asked me what this Joe Baker is like at Torino, I said: 'If you can get him, GET him!' Joe Baker was all that you read about and more – he was dashing, the Roy of the Rovers of his generation. Joe was the finest finisher that I played with, ever."

Joe also made a big impression on David Court, an 18-year-old in the Highbury youth ranks. "He obviously had a mixed time out in Torino, but Joe was a big signing for Arsenal," he says. "He was as brave as a lion, a bit of a gunslinger and he must've been hard to mark. Off the pitch, he very quickly endeared himself to the younger elements of the club. He was a mixer. He had no airs or graces about him – he was one of the boys. Everybody recognised his talent but they liked him as a person too. Some of the most talented players aren't that likeable, but he was. There was no arrogance about Joe and that's what he took with him into the dressing room. He was a very funny, witty person and he was someone we all looked up to and recognised as a real talent."

As well as being a hit with his new team-mates, Joe took an instant liking to English football. Jon Spurling, author of *Rebels for the Cause: the Alternative History of Arsenal Football Club*, wrote of Joe: "With his Elvis quiff, ready smile and fearless play in and around the box, he instantly became a crowd favourite." Joe scored in his first two games, in victories over Leyton Orient and Birmingham City. "Suddenly I had space, nobody was spitting at me and I was allowed to play," he said. "No wonder I scored goals."

Law, who scored on his debut for Manchester United, was equally de-lighted with this new-found freedom – particularly when he bagged four against Ipswich Town. "As much as Joe and I didn't like Italy, I was glad we went because it gave us a lot of experience," he says. "We were definitely better players for having gone there. It was so defensive. We were basically marked with two people on Joe and two people on me and then we came back to England and we felt we weren't being marked at all."

The former team-mates would need to wait before they came up against each other, however, as Joe was injured for the visit of United. The 3-1 defeat marked the beginning of a run of only one win in nine matches for Arsenal before Joe, who already had six goals to his name, was injured again for the trip to White Hart Lane. Joe's injury turned out to be great news for young Court who, in only his third appearance for the club, was handed the shirt of their new ace striker.

He recalls: "It was one of the great pleasures of my life to play alongside Joe. In my second game, against Fulham, he smashed in a volley from outside the box. What a goal. Just to be on the same pitch as someone like that, it gave you the enthusiasm to play with them more and more and to get better."

Joe's influence certainly seemed to have the desired effect on the teenager, who scored twice against Bill Nicholson's double winners in a thrilling 4-4 draw. "Billy Wright told me afterwards that I would keep my place, but I was dropped for Joe coming back," he says. "Joe told me, 'I wouldn't have picked me after the game you just played.' But that's the kind of guy Joe was."

It didn't take Joe long to show he was worthy of his place, however, scoring six goals in the first three games following his return. A 5-4 victory at home to Wolves, which saw Joe score his first hat-trick for the Gunners, and a 5-5 draw away to Blackburn, during which he netted a brace, typified both what was right, and what was wrong, with Billy Wright's side.

"We had a very good forward line, with Joe and with Geoff Strong, who also scored a lot of goals," says Eastham. "I used to slide the ball through and they looked for one-twos with me. They gave me a pass and I'd push it back in for them. You found Joe and Geoff very easily in the box. Joe had good movement and he was a very good player. If it weren't for our defence, you'd think we'd have been challenging for the title."

By Christmas, Joe had hit 16 league goals – more than twice the number he had scored in a season in Italy, but he and his fellow forwards were finding it a constant battle to stay in the ascendancy. Just before the Big Freeze of 1962-63 brought the English football calendar to a grinding halt, Joe's brace in a 2-0 win over Leyton Orient on 15 December managed to put Arsenal back in the black – if only just. They sat ninth in the table, having scored 43 goals but conceded 42.

Joe appeared on the pitch at Old Trafford for the first time in his career on 22 December, but the match was abandoned after an hour due to fog. With Joe in dazzling form for his new club, Sonia made a dazzling bride on 7 January, when she married Joe at St Patrick's Church in Craigneuk. Gerry, naturally, was best man.

The couple were forced to put their honeymoon plans on hold, however, to allow Joe to take part in something of a slightly less romantic nature – the third round FA Cup tie against Fourth Division Oxford United. Already postponed once, the match was again called off and not played until 30 January, with the new groom enjoying his FA Cup bow by scoring twice in a 5-1 win.

After negotiating their way past Sheffield Wednesday in the next round, Arsenal's short FA Cup run was brought to an end by the newly promoted Liverpool, which had another Motherwell lad, Ian St John, leading the line. An unpredictable defence meant that league results were mixed, but Joe's six goals in the last four games of the season, including one in a 3-2 victory over Manchester United at Old Trafford and a hat-trick in the 3-0 win over Fulham, helped haul Arsenal into seventh. Nobody knew it at the time, but the club's league positions would get no better under Billy Wright.

At the end of his debut season in English football, Joe had scored 29 league goals and another two in the FA Cup, tying with Geoff Strong with 31 strikes in all competitions. In May, Arsenal welcomed Rangers to Highbury for a testimonial for their long-serving goalkeeper Jack Kelsey, who had been forced to retire through injury.

With Northern Irishman Jack McClelland having taken over the No.1 shirt and Scot Ian McKechnie as reserve, Arsenal paid Wolves £6,500 for the services of a 21-year-old amateur who would go on to become a Highbury legend. Schoolteacher Bob Wilson signed for Arsenal on 16 July 1963. Before the future double-winner could line up with the professionals, however, the 5ft 8in centre-forward who had signed exactly a year earlier would be forced to go in goal.

Arsenal had lost their opening game of the season at home to Wolves, but Joe had scored twice in the 3-2 win over West Brom. The third match saw them travel to Filbert Street, where Leicester went into an early 2-0 lead. Things got considerably worse in the 22nd minute, when McClelland was injured and, of all people, Joe was the man who volunteered to take his place. "I remember that so well," says Wilson. "I was watching the game and Joe looked like a midget when he took over in goal, especially when you consider that these days all goalkeepers have got to be 6 foot 5. Joe let in five and we lost 7-2, but it was hilarious!"

No match for opposite number Gordon Banks, England's new custodian, Joe soon got back to what he did best, scoring six goals in four consecutive victories. This included a hat-trick against Aston Villa as well as the winner as Manchester United were beaten 2-1 at Highbury.

Three days later, 25 September, marked an historic day for Arsenal. Their first-leg Inter-Cities Fairs Cup tie away to Staevnet was their very first match in Europe. Gerry had been among the scorers when Hibs comfortably beat the Danes the previous season, and it turned out to be a gentle introduction to continental competition for Arsenal as they ran out 7-1 winners. Johnny MacLeod, who put the visitors 1-0 up after only nine minutes, beat Joe to the distinction of being the club's first goalscorer in

Europe by quarter of an hour, but Joe at least had the honour of bagging their first European hat-trick.

Joe and Geoff Strong, who also scored three against Staevnet, were in sensational form. By the time league leaders Spurs visited Highbury on 15 October, Strong had 13 goals to his name, while Joe had scored 15 – the same number as Jimmy Greaves. Arsenal had an impressive home record going into the game, having dropped only two points in six games at Highbury. They were just one point behind Spurs, and had the chance to go top of the table with a win. Joe had missed the 4-4 draw against Tottenham the previous season, but he couldn't have predicted that he was about to play in another.

Greaves put Spurs ahead after only three minutes before Bobby Smith doubled the lead. An Eastham penalty made it 2-1 before Dave MacKay restored Spurs' three-goal cushion. Eastham again reduced the deficit before Smith got his second. With only five minutes remaining and Spurs 4-2 up, Joe set Tottenham nerves jangling when he shot left-footed past Bill Brown, and Strong made them furious by heading the equaliser deep into injury time. Once again, it was clear that Arsenal's main problems lay in defence, and things took a turn for the worse against Aston Villa, when goalkeeper McKechnie picked up an injury. This forced Wright into drastic measures – putting an amateur in goal against Nottingham Forest.

"I was a university boy straight out of Loughborough and I turned up in the Arsenal dressing room wearing a duffle coat and a college scarf – big mistake," says Wilson. "During my first year at Highbury I was actually teaching every day and then I had to train in the evening. So I was an amateur schoolteacher playing in goal for the Arsenal. Of course, most of the players didn't accept me and one of the only ones who did was Joe Baker. He was the only one who understood my discomfort.

"There were other people there who wouldn't even converse with me, including George Eastham, the captain. For him, it was the equivalent now of Wayne Rooney turning round and seeing an amateur schoolteacher in goal, so I understand where they were coming from, but it's bloody hard when you're coming from my background and everything. It was very hard to take. So even when I made my debut against Nottingham Forest, on that day the only one to really put his arm around me and say, 'Come on, enjoy it,' and do his best to make me feel comfortable was Joe Baker. I think he understood what was going through my mind and, for that, I'll always be grateful."

Despite some of the players' reservations, Arsenal lost only one of the six matches they played with Wilson in goal, including the 1-1 draw against

Belgium's Standard Liege in the second round of the Fairs Cup. The club's first European adventure came to an end with a 3-1 defeat in the second leg in Belgium on 18 December, a match Joe missed through injury.

By the end of the year, Joe had scored 22 league goals, closely followed by Strong with 20. Both had played significant roles in the fact Arsenal were fourth in the table, only three points behind leaders Blackburn. For Joe, there was much to be optimistic about, not least because Sonia was due to give birth to their first child in the new year. When she gave birth in the William Smellie Memorial Hospital in Lanark on 17 January 1964, a great deal was made in the newspapers of the fact that Paul Joseph Baker might one day do something his father never could.

"THE BABY WHO CAN PLAY FOR SCOTLAND!" ran the headline on the front page of the *Daily Record*. "It's the chance I never got," said a delighted Joe, with newspapers suggesting that he had insisted on a Scottish birth for his child to ensure he wouldn't be tied to playing for England. Sonia, on the other hand, gave a slightly more truthful, but less headline-friendly reason for being in Scotland to have her baby. "I just wanted to be with my own family – in case Joe had to be away from our home when the baby was born," she said. "I don't know anyone else down there very well."

The new father celebrated with a goal against Fulham before meeting his son for the first time. After knocking West Brom out of the FA Cup, Arsenal were drawn at home to Liverpool for the second year running. Ian St John scored the only goal of the game after 15 minutes, but the main talking point wasn't the football, but rather the boxing match that broke out on the half-hour mark. Few people would ever try to get on the wrong side of Ron Yeats, Liverpool's burly 6ft 2ins centre half, but Joe's fiery temper more than made up for his lack of height. According to David Court, a clash between the two players led his former team-mate to deliver, in the words of one boxing promoter, "one of the best punches he'd ever seen".

"Joe could've been a good boxer if he'd taken to that sport, he was a tough boy," adds Court, who was watching the match from the sidelines. "It was a frustrating game for us and nothing we did was making much headway. Joe just turned round and smacked him and knocked Ron to the ground. They both got sent off, but Ron was still groggy when he walked off."

Yeats had the last laugh, however. On 18 April, Liverpool trounced Arsenal 5-0 at Anfield to secure their first championship under Bill Shankly, a victory that would kick-start nearly two decades of dominance in the English game. Arsenal, meanwhile, were moving in the other direction. Despite their early promise, Billy Wright's side finished eighth.

It certainly wasn't for the want of trying. Joe had more than proved himself in English football. After two seasons at Highbury, he had scored 61 goals in only 87 games. But neither Arsenal's woes nor his own personal glory seemed important to Joe shortly afterwards. Four days after the defeat to Liverpool, Arsenal travelled to Dublin for a friendly. After the game, a call came into the hotel. Joe had to fly back to London to be with Sonia. Their son, Paul Baker, the boy Joe hoped would one day play for Scotland, was dead.

Paul had fallen ill before Joe left for Ireland, but his death hit the couple hard. At least the end of the season allowed Joe to be at home with his wife for a few weeks. But it wasn't long before he was off again, this time for Arsenal's tour of South Africa. Whatever was going through his mind, Joe didn't let it affect his performances on the pitch. He scored six times during the tour and, on the opening day of the 1964-65 season, he had the privilege of starring alongside his team-mates in the very first edition of a new television programme called *Match of the Day*.

Broadcast on the fledgling BBC2 at 6.30pm on 22 August 1964, the highlights of Arsenal's visit to Anfield, or "Beatleville" as it was described by presenter Kenneth Wolstenholme, were watched by only 20,000 people, but Joe played his part in a five-goal thriller that helped to launch a football institution.

"Many people think that this could be Arsenal's year," said Wolstenholme, his ability to see into the future apparently not on a par with his commentating. Although Joe was beaten to the distinction of being the first player to score on *Match of the Day* by Roger Hunt, which was followed by goals from Gordon Wallace and Geoff Strong, his brilliant stooping header for Arsenal's equaliser produced the best commentary of the debut show: "What a beautiful goal! Glorious goal by Baker," screamed Wolstenholme. Wallace struck again for a last-gasp Liverpool winner, but at least Joe and company were spared the modern half-hour, pun-laden, post-match analysis.

A good thing, too. By the end of the season, Alan Hansen might well have run out of words with which to deride Arsenal's defence. Joe, an ever-present in the league campaign for the first time, scored another 25 goals, but a lowly 13th place in the league and getting knocked out of the FA Cup by Third Division Peterborough was stretching the patience of the fans, not to mention Joe.

Gerry doesn't mince his words when it comes to the Arsenal team under Billy Wright. "You only need to look at Joe's record to see that he was good enough to play for any of the top teams and instead he signed for Arsenal, who were crap," he says. "The forward line, including Joe, were scoring all these goals and never once looked like winning anything. I couldn't believe he was playing in a team like that. It wasn't like more recent Arsenal teams. If he was in that team now, crikey, they would break a world record, but he just found playing under Billy Wright incredibly frustrating."

Wilson adds: "Joe was one of our star players at a time when goalscoring for Arsenal wasn't a problem – we scored for fun. We'd score two, three, but we'd let in four. Thankfully I wasn't in the side so it didn't reflect on me."

And despite the respect Joe had for Billy Wright the player, the strain of playing under Wright the manager was beginning to show. Frank McLintock, who signed for Arsenal in 1964 and later captained the double-winning side of 1971, recalled a 1965 pre-season friendly in Jamaica where Joe "got so fed up with Billy Wright's hectoring, half-time team talk that he flung his boots at the manager and refused to go out for the second half".

Joe, who during that West Indies tour scored six goals in a match against one of the local sides, soon found himself facing the wrath of the Jamaican public. The bad-tempered deciding match of the tri-team Independence Soccer Festival that involved Arsenal, Trinidad and the hosts lasted only 37 minutes. Howls of derision rained down from the stands in Kingston after Joe felled a Jamaican defender, but the boos turned into bottles after Alan Skirton put Arsenal 2-0 up and then Lascelles Dunckley, the Jamaica captain, was sent off along with McLintock. When play eventually resumed, it didn't last long when Joe, squaring up to Jamaica defender Frank Brown, whipped the crowd into a frenzy. With the pitch, according to one report, now "a glass-littered boxing arena", the referee was forced to abandon the match.

Court reveals that Joe's experiences in Italy came in useful as the players planned their escape from the stadium. "Joe had seen the Italian riots first hand, particularly after scoring the winner against Juventus, and he warned us to make sure we put our coats over our heads as we got into the bus," he says.

Wilson adds: "The crowd were so built up to beat the mighty Arsenal and after going two goals down they went mad, they wouldn't accept it. But Joe again showed that he had an amazing fiery temperament beneath that shy exterior."

Thousands of miles away, in a hospital ward in Glasgow, Sonia Baker was listening to reports of the drama on the radio. She was concerned, but good news awaited Joe. His wife had just given birth to a healthy baby girl, Nadia. "This baby means very much to them after what happened," said Sonia's mother Victoria. "The birth of Nadia will help them both very much."

The joy of this new addition to the Baker family was special to Joe, but the 1965-66 season saw on-field frustrations continue, although the striker did reach another personal landmark. On 28 December, Arsenal's fifth goal against Sheffield Wednesday marked Joe's century for Arsenal – it was his 93rd in the league in only 141 matches. Prior to this, only Newcastle United legend Hughie Gallacher had scored 100 goals on both sides of the Border, while Joe was only the third player since the War to reach the milestone in an Arsenal shirt.

But a total of 100 goals in 156 appearances in his three and a half seasons at Highbury barely seems to register among some Arsenal fans. His image does not grace the outside of the new Emirates Stadium, while the book, *Arsenal – The Official Illustrated History 1886-2010*, awards him but a solitary sentence on page 103.

Joe, like George Eastham, had the misfortune of leaving Arsenal empty-handed, gracing Highbury in the only decade since the 1920s – and since – that the club failed to win a trophy. For those who played alongside him, however, Joe's performances in the red and white will live long in the memory.

"Joe Baker, in particular, was a phenomenal player," wrote Frank McLintock in his autobiography. "He was all you could want in a goalscorer – equally adept with both feet and with the sort of pace that Ian Rush later used to such advantage. I love players like Joe, with the economical pace of Jimmy Greaves, the short back-lift when they shoot and the bravery that distinguishes the great from the merely good."

Wilson, who admired Joe as a person as well as a player, adds: "Joe Baker, without any doubt, is right up there among Arsenal's greatest ever strikers. When it comes to scoring goals for Arsenal you have to put Thierry Henry at the top, closely followed by Ian Wright. I would then immediately jump to Joe Baker. I loved Joe."

Joe was frustrated by the fact that the Highbury goalscoring machine, of which he was the main component, failed to win any silverware. There was more to life, however. After leaving Italy, Joe explained that one reason he was looking forward to playing at Highbury was the chance to resurrect his England career.

"I aim to get back into that white shirt with the No. 9 on the back," he said. "That'll be worth more to me than all the big bonuses." But by the time the call eventually came, there was a new man at the helm – a man who had been charged with delivering to England fans the greatest trophy of all.

16
Taking on the World

While 30 July 1966 is undoubtedly the most significant date in the history of English football, 25 October 1962 is perhaps equally notable. This was the day that Alf Ramsey, the manager of Ipswich Town, accepted the Football Association's offer to take charge of the national team. It was also a good day for Joe Baker who, now back on British soil and having got his Arsenal career off to a flying start, would finally find himself back in contention for an England place.

A lot had happened to the 22-year-old since his last involvement at international level. His last memory of representing England, in October 1960, had involved an angry Italian mob, furious that his shoulder-charged effort in their Under-23 clash at St James' Park had been allowed to stand. Perhaps Joe should have taken this as a sign of things to come before moving to Turin.

Due to Hibs' league fixture against St Johnstone on the same day, Joe was overlooked for the next Under-23 game – against Wales on 8 February 1961 – in favour of Johnny "Budgie" Byrne. But despite the Crystal Palace star's impressive performance in the 2-0 win, the selectors couldn't ignore Joe's explosive form – particularly his two goals at the Nou Camp against Barcelona. And, having been denied the chance to play in the fixture the previous year due to Hibs' Scottish Cup commitments, Joe was delighted to be chosen to wear the No. 9 shirt against Scotland Under-23s on 1 March, not least because a good showing in Middlesbrough might boost his chances of a recall to the senior side. It wouldn't be easy. Since taking Joe's place in the line-up after the disappointing summer tour of 1960, Spurs' Bobby Smith had scored six times in four consecutive England victories. Ever the optimist, however, Joe was certain that he was good enough to win back his place.

But with Hibs still far from safe in the fight against relegation, the club asked the FA for permission to play Joe in their re-arranged league fixture against Airdrie on the evening of 27 February. Agreeing to Hibs' request but sticking rigidly to their principle – as they had a year previously – of not considering a player who had turned out for his club immediately prior to an international, the FA promptly dropped Joe for the match against

Scotland and reinstated Byrne. And, in keeping with the behaviour of an association that would later ignore a letter from their own World Cup-winning captain, Bobby Moore, when he wrote them a letter offering his services, the men at Lancaster Gate neglected to inform either Hibs or Joe that this would be the case.

"I am fed up with the whole affair. It is absolutely ridiculous," said Joe, after he had scored a sublime third goal in Hibs' 3-3 draw with Airdrie. "I don't know whether I will be travelling to England or not. I am still prepared to go, but I just don't know where I stand. Like Hibs, I have heard nothing officially."

Joe didn't play against Scotland and, with hindsight, he probably would have done well not to speak out. Aside from Joe replacing Byrne when the Palace striker was a late call-off for the match against the seniors on 5 May, Byrne remained in the side until after Joe moved to Italy, by which time he had disappeared out of the international picture. Until 1962, England named only one reserve per match and, even when this was increased to three – sometimes five – competition for places was always fierce.

A chink of light emerged for Joe, now at Arsenal, when it came time for England to select a squad of 22 players for a European Cup of Nations qualifier. The competition that would become known as the European Championships was to be held for only the second time in 1964 and England had been paired with France. After drawing the first game 1-1 at home in October 1962, Ramsey would oversee his very first England match for the return leg in Paris on 27 February 1963.

He was not due to start his post officially until May but, despite the threat of relegation hanging over Ipswich, it was agreed that he could accompany the team to Paris. This particular group of England players was significant, as it was the last to be chosen by committee. From that moment on, who played for England and who didn't would be Ramsey's decision, and his decision alone.

Exactly one year on from his brush with death on the streets of Turin and having just moved into his first house together with his new wife, Joe was elated to be named in the squad. It seemed, too, that he had a good chance of taking to the field in Paris. Alan Peacock, who had scored twice in England's last game, the 4-0 win over Wales at Wembley, was injured and, as far as the selectors were concerned, there were only two viable replacements – Bobby Smith and Joe Baker.

Like Joe, Smith had recently found himself in the international wilderness. Following the 2-0 defeat to Scotland in April 1962, the only time in seven matches he had ended up on the losing side, he was dropped in favour of Gerry Hitchens. Smith hadn't played since and, prior to Christmas, he had also been finding it difficult to get a game for Spurs.

Almost as though scripted, the two strikers were scheduled to do battle in the North London derby four days before the big kick-off in Paris. With two England selectors among the 60,000 crowd at Highbury, it was pure football theatre – a duel for the right to play against France.

"Joe is just the type England need," said Arsenal manager Billy Wright, his money firmly on his man ahead of the Saturday kick-off. "He's quick to react and more used to playing against Continental massed defences. France are likely to mass in defence more than usual in Paris, and Joe is more likely to break down that sort of game."

Joe, meanwhile, was more relaxed. "It sounds crazy, but I really don't care if Bobby Smith beats me to that England centre-forward spot against France," he said. "It seems certain the state of the ground will determine the lucky leader, so there will be no reflection on the one left out. People often say it's the thought that counts and for me it's enough to know I'm back in the England reckoning."

Playing on a snow-covered surface, Smith seemed to have made the selectors' tricky decision a mite easier just before half-time when he fired Spurs into the lead with a spectacular volley. And although Joe shot home from a difficult angle late in the game, Spurs won the match 3-2 and, with it, their striker had won his fight to reclaim his England place.

Joe was subsequently named as one of four reserves for what turned out to be a disastrous 5-2 defeat to the French. The home side were 3-0 up at half-time, but Smith vindicated his selection by taking his enviable international record to nine goals in only eight matches.

Ramsey shook things up for the visit of Scotland to a newly refurbished Wembley on 6 April, making five changes, but it didn't stop Smith keeping Joe out the team, nor did it stop Jim Baxter, in the words of debutant England goalkeeper Gordon Banks, "strolling arrogantly around Wembley as if he owned the place" and scoring twice in a 2-1 win.

Despite Joe's 31 goals in his first season at Arsenal, he was not part of England's successful 1963 summer tour, during which an increasingly confident Ramsey had gone from suggesting that England had "a wonderful chance", to insisting that they "will win" the 1966 World Cup.

It wasn't until the historic occasion of Wednesday 23 October 1963 that Joe was involved with England again. To celebrate its centenary, the Football Association had arranged a match between England and a star-studded Rest of the World XI. Unlike later incarnations of the World XI that come together in the name of Soccer Aid, which has seen the likes of Mike Myers,

Woody Harrelson and Alistair Campbell turn out for the visiting team, the side that took on Ramsey's men was comprised of bona fide football legends. Captained by Alfredo di Stefano, the Rest of the World featured players such as Russia's Lev Yashin, Eusebio of Portugal, Raymond Kopa of France and, naturally, Joe's old flat-mate Denis Law.

Joe, meanwhile, had to content himself with a place on the bench. Substitutes were permitted, but he could only watch in envy as opposition coach Fernando Riera made four changes to his side at half-time, including the introduction of 36-year-old Hungarian magician Ferenc Puskas, while Ramsey stuck steadfastly to his starting XI until the final whistle. England beat the Rest of the World 2-1, and now Ramsey would be going all out to ensure they beat the world to the sport's ultimate prize in three years' time. Joe had twice come close to playing for England again and had twice ended up disappointed. He could, however, take heart from the fact that this time it had been Ramsey, not a team of selectors, who had put him in the squad.

It was a crumb of comfort and, even as Joe left Wembley Stadium without making so much as a two-minute cameo, he couldn't have imagined that many more months and, in the end, two years, would elapse before Ramsey would pick him again.

"When Joe got recalled to the England team, it was amazing, it was a miracle," says Gerry. But perhaps the only miracle about Joe's call-up to train with the squad in November 1965, only eight months before England were set to host the eighth World Cup, was that it hadn't come sooner. Joe had recently scored his 96th goal for Arsenal in the space of three and a half seasons when he was chosen to play in a "Shadow England XI", alongside Alan Ball and Roger Hunt, for a practice match against Ramsey's side as they prepared to face Northern Ireland in the Home Championship at Wembley on 10 November. England and Ramsey were still not using the system that they would employ in the World Cup – and subsequently – of naming a starting XI on the day of a match, rather than selecting the side a week beforehand and hoping that injury or illness wouldn't strike in the meantime.

Fortunately for Joe on this occasion, however, that optimism was misplaced. Jimmy Greaves, a shoo-in for any England line-up at inside-right, spent the weekend before the match in bed with flu. Greaves missed Spurs' defeat against Nottingham Forest while, at the same time, Ramsey was at Highbury watching Joe score twice in Arsenal's 6-2 demolition of Sheffield United. Blackpool youngster Ball was another contender but, when Greaves made his inevitable withdrawal from the squad, Ramsey had already made up his mind.

Joe recalled: "After the last training session Alf called me over and said 'I need a man for No. 8 – do you think you could do the job for me?' I wondered what he thought, but naturally said 'Yes'. He answered: 'It's yours – you play tonight.'"

Just after his selection, Joe said: "All these years I have never given up hope that I might play for England again. I'm really thrilled. I've kept trying, kept playing, now I have made it. I know I have to take over Jimmy's job, and I haven't played there before, but there is more room to work at inside forward. This is my best season."

Joe might have been playing in an unfamiliar position under a different manager, but the rebirth of his international career bore so many similarities to where it had all begun for him as a 19-year-old exactly six years earlier – the same competition, the same venue, the same opposition, albeit one that now included a teenage superstar called George Best. But the world had changed. When Joe first turned out for England, Cliff Richard was top of the UK charts – this time round it was a bunch of young upstarts called the Rolling Stones who were commanding people to "get off of my cloud". Since he last pulled on an England shirt, the national side had played more than 50 matches without Joe Baker. But now, against all the odds, he had a chance to show them what they had been missing.

By this stage, Ramsey's line-up was fast turning into the one that would become so familiar the following summer – and indeed for the next 50 years. Gordon Banks was in goal, with George Cohen and Ray Wilson as the full-backs and Nobby Stiles, Jack Charlton and Bobby Moore across the middle. Peter Thompson of Liverpool and John Connelly, now with Manchester United, were the wide men, while centre-forward Alan Peacock was supported by Bobby Charlton at inside-left and Joe at inside-right.

As Joe looked around at his England team-mates, none of whom had played the last time he appeared in this fixture, the day he stepped into a taxi at London Airport as a fresh-faced teenager must have seemed a lifetime ago. He had been through so much, including playing alongside each and every one of Hibs' Famous Five, that it was hard to believe Joe had only recently turned 25. And, exactly as he had done six years earlier, he took less than 20 minutes to show the 70,000-strong crowd, in the words of his big brother, exactly "why they picked a fucking Scotsman to play for England".

On the edge of the area, Joe shaped to pass to Peacock with his right foot before pulling the ball back and firing past the helpless Pat Jennings with his left. Willie Irvine made it 1-1 as the crowd were still celebrating, but Joe turned provider for Peacock in the 72nd minute. Scored one, made one, a 2-1 victory over Northern Ireland. It was as though Joe had never been away. The team's overall performance had been far from convincing, but the *Daily Mail* ran with the headline: "Baker must stay". It was a call Ramsey heeded, not that the England manager needed anyone else's advice, for England's match against Spain in the Bernabeu on 8 December.

Although only a friendly, the game turned out to be one of the most significant of Ramsey's reign – it was the night his side utterly outclassed the European champions, a night when the whole country could truly believe the manager's bold claim that England could win the World Cup.

Instead of the traditional 4-2-4, Ramsey decided to take a risk, by deploying the 4-3-3 formation he had used in a 2-1 victory over Sweden. He felt attacking through the middle would give England the best chance of victory over the Spanish but, as things transpired, it was a match that convinced Ramsey that using a formation without wide men was the way forward. It was the night that his "Wingless Wonders" took flight.

In front of Banks, the defence consisted of Cohen, Jack Charlton, Moore and Wilson; in midfield were Bobby Charlton, Stiles and Joe's Arsenal team-mate George Eastham. With Greaves now suffering from hepatitis, Liverpool striker Roger Hunt formed a three-pronged attack alongside Alan Ball and Joe. As the match kicked off, England were acutely aware of the fact that they had never won on Spanish soil, which during that match was covered with melting snow.

Joe's last experience of playing Spain, alongside Charlton and Wilson in the summer of 1960, was a miserable one as England were beaten 3-0. This time, desperate to play, Joe was harbouring a secret – one that he wouldn't reveal until five years later. He explained: "Two days before we were due to fly out I pulled a muscle training at Highbury. For the next 48 hours I tried to convince myself that it was only minor damage and that got me on the plane. The England training out there was negligible so I was never put to the test. Nobody twigged – not even the rest of the players. But when I sat in the dressing room before the kick-off I knew I had done wrong. I could still feel a nagging pain in my calf muscle, and England took the field with ten fit players."

Struggling through pain that felt "as though someone was sawing off a leg" Joe was able to stay on the pitch only half an hour, but he needed only eight minutes, for the second match in succession, to put England into the lead. After a quickly taken free-kick by Eastham, Wilson fired in a hard, low cross, which Joe side-footed into the net from four yards. The remainder of his time on the pitch was "a nightmare of pain" and it was clear he would have to come off.

Joe had already made international football history by becoming the first player outside the Football League to turn out for England. In Madrid he made history again, although not in a way he would have wanted – Ramsey pushed Bobby Charlton forward as Joe made way for Norman Hunter of Leeds United, who became the first England player to make his debut as a substitute.

Joe was only the ninth England player in 15 years to be replaced. Sven Goran Eriksson would make more changes than that in the space of 45 minutes. Hunter had Joe's deception to thank for winning his first England cap, but the man he replaced wasn't proud of what he had done.

"I was unfair to England, to Sir Alf and to myself," said Joe later. "The only excuse I can plead is that I was desperate to get into the England set-up for the World Cup."

England, in one of their best performances for years, tore the Spanish apart. Hunt doubled England's lead in the second half to give Ramsey's men a 2-0 win, but it was clear that a scoreline of 5-0 or even 6-0 would not have flattered the visitors. Following the match, Spain coach Jose Villalonga named England as his favourites to win the World Cup.

Desmond Hackett, the *Daily Express* reporter who had waxed lyrical about Joe following his debut in 1959, wholeheartedly agreed. "England can win the World Cup next year," he gushed. "They have only to match the splendour of this unforgettable night and there is not a team on earth who could master them."

Although pleased with the result, the England squad would be taking Hackett's words with a large pinch of salt, especially as, not even a month earlier, he had announced: "England are not even the best team in England."

Still, the effect of the switch in tactics was obvious, with Bobby Charlton saying: "It was comical to see them wasting their time because we often had five players going through the middle and never had five forwards strung out across the field."

Ramsey said later: "I think really this was when it first registered firmly in my mind as a system that could win the World Cup."

A system, but not all of the players. On 23 December, the manager announced a 22-man squad for what would be England's first game of the World Cup year. The team would be playing an international virtually every month to give Ramsey the chance to finalise his selection. For the match against Poland on 5 January – the first meeting between the two countries at senior level – Ramsey called up five uncapped players, one of whom would be particularly significant, not only for England, but for Joe personally.

The new faces were Keith Newton (Blackburn), Paul Reaney (Leeds), Gordon Harris (Burnley), John Kaye (West Brom) and a young striker who had already bagged 22 goals for West Ham that season – Geoff Hurst.

Five days after the England squad was announced, Joe, now recovered from his pulled muscle, notched up his 100th – and last – goal for Arsenal in a 5-2 win over Sheffield Wednesday. He kept his place against Poland, with the only change in the side being Harris coming in for the injured Bobby Charlton. The match would be played at Everton's Goodison Park, one of the World Cup venues. Joe took the train from London to Liverpool with Ramsey, Moore, Eastham, Cohen and newcomer Hurst, who admitted that he had been "flabbergasted" to be called into the squad.

But, following the euphoria of the win against Spain, the 1-1 draw with the Poles, who hadn't even qualified for the World Cup, was seen as a major setback. Playing on a muddy pitch, it was clear England badly missed Charlton. Joe did nothing of note, with England's equaliser coming from an unlikely source in Bobby Moore.

The following day, the World Cup groups were announced and England now had only seven matches to play before they kicked off their campaign against Uruguay. Ramsey made three changes for the next match, against West Germany on 23 February, and the team sheet didn't made good reading for Joe, who had since moved to Nottingham Forest. While Newton came in for Wilson at left-back, Hunter replaced Eastham in midfield and Joe's place up front was taken by Hurst. Curiously, it was actually Stiles who was wearing Hurst's usual No.10 jersey, and it was the Manchester United terrier who scored the only goal in a 1-0 win. Stiles himself was a big admirer of Joe, saying, "Baker was quick and intelligent and perfectly suited to Ramsey's concept of a well-organised but also extremely fluid England team."

But it was prophetic that Hurst, who would become the scorer of arguably the most famous hat-trick in world football, should make his England debut against West Germany at Wembley, although the fact that Stiles was playing up front was a clear sign that Ramsey had not yet settled on his final line-up.

Hurst wasn't convinced he had done enough. Of his performance against the Germans he remarked: "The best I can say is that I made no serious mistakes." But he retained his place for England's next game, scoring his first international goal in a thrilling 4-3 win over Scotland at Hampden.

But all was not lost for Joe. FIFA required each team to submit a preliminary list of 40 players by 28 May. Ramsey would then have until eight days before the start of the World Cup to give the organisers a final squad of 22. It was a protracted process that must have played havoc with the nerves of England's finest as, curiously, the final squad didn't have to contain a single player from the original list.

The well-organised Ramsey named his initial 40-man squad nearly two months ahead of schedule, on 7 April, in order to give clubs as much notice as possible. Joe was on the list, but the England manager also called up two more uncapped youngsters: Peter Osgood, of Chelsea, and Martin Peters of West Ham.

On 6 May, the FA made another announcement, naming 28 players to report to Lilleshall for 11 days' training ahead of a pre-tournament tour consisting of warm-up matches against Finland, Norway, Denmark and Poland. On the same day, Ramsey also announced three changes to the squad of 40. Joe was still on the list but, unlike Hurst, he was not selected to report for training at Lilleshall. Instead, he was put on stand-by.

Only 27 players went to Lilleshall as Brian Labone withdrew with an injury. At the end of the training period, Ramsey took five of the players aside to tell them they would not be going on tour. It has been written that all hope was lost for those left behind but, in theory, any player in England – even one that had not been named in the original list of 40 – could have been named in the final squad.

Realistically, for Joe and the rest of those staying in England, however, the writing was on the wall. And so it proved. On 3 July, when Ramsey officially announced the men he would be taking to the World Cup, only the 22 players on tour were in the final squad. Of these, only three forwards – Hunt, Hurst and Greaves – would get to play for England on the biggest stage of all.

"I don't know what happened. I just disappeared out of the picture," said Joe later. "That's what I didn't like about Ramsey, that he didn't explain things man to man. If he'd said, 'Look Joe, I've decided on the system I'm playing and I think Roger and Jimmy play it best, I'm the one who gets the stick if it fails, so I am sorry I can't have you,' I could accept that, but not to get a call or a letter was awful. Like all managers he had his favourites, and my face didn't fit. Maybe he didn't like my accent!"

But while Ramsey was said to have a dislike for "Scotch bastards", as he was heard to describe the Scots during England versus Scotland team talks, Joe knew that his omission had less to do with the way he talked and more to do with his five goals in 14 games in a struggling Nottingham Forest side. It was hardly the kind of return that people had come to expect from the great Joe Baker.

George Eastham, still at Arsenal, picked up a World Cup-winner's medal, albeit many years after the 4-2 win over West Germany, after being named in Ramsey's final 22. He says: "When you look at the England team in that fantastic victory over Spain, me and Joe were the only players that weren't on the pitch when they won the World Cup. That shows you how just how unlucky you can be."

"I was sick watching England win the World Cup," admitted Joe. "I was pleased for the lads, because I knew them so well, but it was hard to take."

One of those lads, now Sir Bobby Charlton, says: "I played alongside Joe for England and for England Under-23s from a young age and I was always struck by his speed and his natural goal-scoring ability – not to mention his broad Scottish accent! The fact that he was able to fight his way back into contention for England after so many years out of the side said a lot for his determination and for his ability. I'm sure Joe would have loved to be part of the World Cup squad, and it was just unfortunate for Joe that he, along with so many other great players, was ultimately left disappointed."

Even though he was still only 25, Joe never played for England again. But while his international career was over, his brother's was yet to begin.

17
Star-spangled Banter

At nearly 1,500ft tall, the Empire State Building remains top of the to-do list for millions of tourists who flock to New York City every year. Back in 1968, it was the tallest free-standing structure in the world. Dominating the city's skyline, it was a symbol of American might that rose amid the ashes of the Great Depression. It raised aspirations, captured the world's imagination and helped to cement the country's status as a superpower.

It seems odd to think, then, that somewhere within this almighty structure lay the national headquarters of a sport in which, in terms of support, income and talent, the USA was utterly impoverished. Soccer was the poor immigrant cousin of baseball, football and basketball. It wasn't so much a case of the world's favourite game playing second fiddle to these sports. Rather, it was left to tinkle away forlornly on the triangle, unable to make itself heard above the orchestral din of the USA's national obsessions.

Despite this, the United States soccer team had enjoyed a result that has echoed down the ages of all-time great upsets, a match that continues to serve as a warning against complacency. On 29 June 1950, Joe Gaetjens, a striker with New York team Brookhattan, scored the winning goal against England in the World Cup – the first time the so-called guardians of the game had entered this global competition. America, a team of part-time players captained and managed by Scotsmen, became overnight heroes, but the momentous result alone was not enough to embed the game within the national consciousness. It certainly didn't encourage youngsters to take up the round ball game in their droves. They remained far more interested in trying to swing a bat like Babe Ruth or score a touchdown like Jim Brown.

What the United States Soccer Football Association (which became the United States Soccer Federation in 1974) needed was more star names, more support and, most importantly, a return to the greatest stage on earth. The 1970 World Cup in Mexico was the immediate goal. When former Wales striker Phil Woosnam was appointed United States head coach in 1968, having brought North American Soccer League glory to the Atlanta Braves, he and his assistant Gordon Jago decided that Gerry Baker, now in the twilight of his career at Coventry City, would be part of these plans.

"During that period, US Soccer, in terms of the national team, was hardly in existence," explains Jago, who played for Charlton Athletic before turning to management. "For example, the national team played only one game in 1959, losing 8-1 against England. They had two games in 1960, both against Mexico, one game in 1964, where they lost 10-0 to England, four games in 1965 and then no more games until 1968. The North American Soccer League (NASL), which was professional, came into being in 1967, but less than a quarter of the players in the league were qualified to represent the national team. The selection of players was very limited.

"We were able to play two matches against Israel prior to the first World Cup qualifier against Canada, but we were really short on experienced forwards and when it was known that Gerry was eligible, every effort was made to have him join the team. We had a long conversation about bringing him over because, at that time, we had to carefully consider the financial side of things. The Association had no money and they were asking Phil and me: 'Is he worth it? Can we afford it?'"

Former US manager Otto Radich had faced similar problems a few years earlier, when he was keen to play Gerry in the qualifiers for World Cup 66, only for the USSFA to baulk at the price of flying him over. Even if the Association had agreed to stump up, it is highly unlikely that Bill McGarry, Gerry's boss at Ipswich Town, would have allowed his striker to miss an entire month of the season to play for the land of his birth. It would be another three years before Gerry's chance came again.

Ipswich were 15th in Division Two in 1965-66, but they made a far better fist of promotion the following season, with Gerry scoring 13 goals in 30 games as the club finished fifth. When Ipswich returned to the top flight at the fourth time of asking, as Second Division champions in 1967-68, Gerry had already beaten them to it. In November 1967, he became one of the first signings made by new Coventry City manager Noel Cantwell. The former Manchester United captain had taken over from Jimmy Hill, who had just led the club through three successive promotions to reach the top flight for the first time in their history.

Hill left the club before the start of the 1967-68 season to concentrate on his television career, leaving Cantwell with the unenviable task, not only of living up to his predecessor's legendary status among the fans, but of keeping Coventry in the First Division. Struggling with only two wins in 14 matches, the manager was forced to dip into the transfer market. He signed his former Manchester United team-mate Maurice Setters for £25,000 from Stoke, then paid Ipswich the same amount for Gerry. Playing mostly as a winger in a struggling side, Gerry's goal count dropped to only five in 23 appearances in the league. But, in a team that ultimately escaped relegation by a single point, his strikes in 1-1 draws against West Ham and Liverpool, and in a 2-1 win over Chelsea, were crucial. The victory over the Blues at Highfield Road was also significant as it featured Coventry's very first "all-Scottish" forward line of Gerry, Willie Carr, Ernie Hannigan, Ian Gibson and Neil Martin, Gerry's former team-mate at Hibs who was making his Coventry debut after signing from Sunderland. The flame-haired Carr, famous for providing a "donkey-kick" assist for Ernie Hunt's volley against Everton in 1970, remembers Gerry as "skilful", "quick", and "always having a smile on his face".

But while Carr's career with the Sky Blues was beginning to take off, the start of the 1968-69 season had seen 30-year-old Gerry reduced to bit-part player. His goal in the 2-1 win at home to Newcastle on 7 September 1968 would be his last in top-flight football, and he would make only seven more appearances for Coventry.

Gerry, who had watched his brother's World Cup dream end in disappointment in 1966, could hardly have believed the news he received three days after the win over Newcastle. "We had just lost 1-0 to Chelsea in a Tuesday night game at Highfield Road," he recalls. "Afterwards, Noel Cantwell called me into his office and told me that the United States Soccer Football Association had asked about my availability for the World Cup qualifiers, which were due to start the next month. I couldn't believe it. After all these years, I'd finally got the call. I was told that, if I was interested, I had to get the plane out to New York from Birmingham early the next morning.

"It was absolutely pissing rain that night, maybe that's why the thought of playing in places like Miami and San Diego sounded so appealing. But I also think Coventry were probably glad to get rid of me. I clearly wasn't in the manager's plans at that stage and they would never have let me go if they thought they had needed me for the next game. The Soccer Association was just beginning to sort itself out then and it wasn't until Phil Woosnam and Gordon Jago took over that they thought 'This boy was born in America, let's give him a chance.'"

Gerry had not even been back to the States since his parents left New Rochelle in 1939, and here he was, three decades later, on the verge of representing the national football team. Arriving at the United States Soccer Football Association headquarters in the Empire State Building, and looking down at the iconic cabs bustling like so many yellow insects on the streets of Manhattan below, Gerry knew that his career was winding down. But the prospect of pulling on an international jersey for the first time gave him a renewed sense of enthusiasm for the game.

"The first thing I was asked after I arrived was whether I had an American passport," he says. "I did, but if I'd said no I'd have been back on that plane and back to Coventry." But with pickings so slim, the USSFA was never going to turn away a man who, after all, was still plying his trade in the English First Division.

"Gerry Baker was the first top-flight European player we had ever had," says Jago. "Because the US Soccer team hardly ever played any games, and because the Association had no money, teams were just assembled – virtually at the last minute. They had nothing and there was no organisation. The team was only brought together occasionally. It was in no way the professional set-up that it is today. The ethnic groups in the major US cities would form football teams, such as the Philadelphia Ukrainians or the New York Greeks. Even in the Seventies, the young American player couldn't play soccer anywhere. There were hardly any playing, even in those ethnic leagues and, in fact, they weren't wanted because they weren't good enough.

"Teams like the Philadelphia Ukrainians had enough Eastern Europeans in that area so that the American boy couldn't play. He was cast aside. That was the problem we experienced. There were very few American players. You had to have two American players on your roster and that was it. There just weren't any American players around, and that's why the US national team hardly played any matches."

German-born Willy Roy, a member of the US Soccer Hall of Fame and the scorer of ten goals in 20 internationals for the States, agrees that the American way wasn't the most professional. "The Association was almost a joke at that time," he says, bluntly. "They would call us up two weeks before games and they would say, 'Are you in shape? We've got a game coming up.' I would say 'I'm in good shape, yeah.' It was totally comical. It also seemed that, every year, we would have a different coach. My first training session with the US national team was in Bermuda in 1965. We had George Meyer and a Hungarian guy from New York coaching us. The trouble was, the Association forgot to tell either one of them who the head coach was before our first practice session – this is no joke. George told us to start jogging, the Hungarian guy said start sprinting, and there was a section of Chicago players who didn't know who to listen to. That's how comical it was. They should have named them co-coaches, but someone at the Association sided with one guy and somebody else sided with the other guy. It was unbelievable. We had an exhibition game in Cleveland and the coach said, 'We've got a lot of injuries, do you know anybody in Chicago who might want to come and play?'"

It was perhaps little wonder, then, that the American public, or at least the small percentage that gave a darn, had been waiting so long for a team to cheer at the World Cup. Since the 1950 tournament in Brazil, the United States had repeatedly seen their return to the competition barred by Mexico. In the four qualifying campaigns since then, the Mexicans had dished out a series of humiliating defeats, which included beating the Americans 7-2 in the very first match between the nations to be played on US soil. But with Mexico qualifying automatically for the 1970 competition as hosts, the American side that contained Gerry Baker were presented with what was arguably their best chance of appearing in a World Cup for 20 years.

It still wouldn't be easy. With only 16 teams set to compete in the final tournament, the 12 members of CONCACAF (the Confederation of North, Central American and Caribbean Association Football), minus Cuba, knew that only one place at football's top table was available. They were divided into four groups of three. In Group 1, the United States would play Canada and Bermuda, with the winner of the group progressing to a two-legged semi-final against the winners of Group 2, which contained Haiti, Guatemala and Trinidad & Tobago.

Before their first qualifier against Canada in October 1968, Woosnam and Jago were determined to whip the US team into some kind of shape. "We did a lot of our training at all the big American Football grounds," explains Gerry. "The American footballers, 6ft 4in giants, who were 16 stone of solid muscle, must have been looking down at us in our wee gutties and our wee shorts thinking 'Who the fuck are these dwarfs?' Over and above the qualifiers, I played about nine games for America against club sides. We had to play matches and keep sharp, so I also appeared as a guest for various teams. On one occasion, we were playing a team up in Canada and we were winning easily, leading 3-1. At half-time, the promoter came in and said, in no uncertain terms, 'If you guys win this, you're not getting any money.' Each of us was on a $150 guest fee so we didn't want to lose out. We let them get back on level terms and then I won a penalty. I ended up putting it over the bar!"

On Gerry's next visit to Canada, however, there would be no question of him trying to miss the target. On 13 October 1968, he lined up with his new team-mates at Varsity Stadium, Toronto, for his United States debut. Amazingly, despite his Lanarkshire accent and living all but one of his 30 years in the UK, Gerry found that he was one of only three members of the American line-up that day – the others being Gary DeLong and Eddie Clear – to have actually been born in the States. Also in the US melting pot to face Canada were Germans Helmut Kofler, Dietrich Albrecht and

Willy Roy, Ukrainian Nick Krat, Yugoslav Siegfried Stritzl, and future USA head coach Bob Gansler, from Hungary. Peter Millar, a Scot playing for New York Inter and with whom Gerry stayed in New Jersey, completed the line-up.

While Joe Baker's hands were tied when it came to international selection, Jago admits that the United States policy wasn't nearly so strict. "They bent the rules quite a bit," he admits. "If any player emerged that they thought they could make a US citizen, then they would go all out to make them a citizen – putting them through the process a bit quicker. It's certainly true that there weren't many American accents in the team at that time."

Gansler says: "Gerry was a good player, and I also remember him as a free-spirited individual. He was easy to like. He had no airs, he was genuine and you could have a beer with him. He didn't say things like, 'Listen you guys, I'm playing in the English First Division and you're just colonists playing *our* sport.' His talent was there, but his demeanour was there as well."

The fact the match against Canada was an important World Cup qualifier was hardly borne out in the attendance. Fewer than 6,000 spectators were in the ground, the home of the collegiate football team the Varsity Blues. Gerry had played in front of bigger crowds in the Scottish Reserve League. And, for someone who, as a young man, had scored in front of more than 100,000 people in the Scottish Cup final, Gerry's international debut was hardly a glamorous occasion. He was also accustomed to having his name spelled correctly in the match programme, with "Gary Baker" making an unexpected appearance. Even less pleasing was the outcome, with the Canadians winning 4-2. Having already beaten Bermuda 4-0 a week earlier, Canada topped the group.

Despite Roy giving the United States the lead, Woosnam's World Cup campaign had got off to the worst possible start and meant his side would have to rely on Bermuda to take points off the Canadians in Hamilton. The re-match between the United States and Canada was scheduled to take place in Atlanta, Georgia, ten days later. Before then, however, Woosnam would take his players even further south – to Port-au-Prince, Haiti, where they would play three friendly matches in just four days. The results would be mixed, but the trip to the land of the fearsome dictator Francois Duvalier, better known to the world as Papa Doc, would at least give the American coach the chance to test his side against their potential semi-final opponents.

In a match in the Estadio Sylvio Cator on 20 October, braces from Millar, Albrecht and Roy gave the United States a 6-3 win, not to mention a timely confidence boost. In retrospect, it might have been a good idea to fly home immediately as, the very next day, the Haitians virtually reversed the score, winning 5-2. Gerry was rested for that game, but returned to the side two days later, with Haiti this time winning 1-0.

"Considering the US played Haiti three times in practically as many days, the crowds were phenomenal," says Gerry. "I remember wondering whether Papa Doc had forced them to go. I also seem to remember that you were flagged offside if you crossed the halfway line!"

If the two nations were to face each other in the semi-finals of qualifying, the result would be a difficult one to call. Papa Doc, never one to miss an opportunity for some political posturing, invited Gerry and the rest of the United States party during their brief stay in Haiti to pay a visit to his luxurious presidential palace. "We were walking in, typical Americans, casual as you like, and then we were pushed up against the wall and searched," recalls Gerry. "The food was pretty good but the politics sucked," adds Gansler.

There was a cruel irony in the invitation to the palace given that, four years earlier, Joe Gaetjens, the Haiti-born striker who became an American hero by knocking the mighty England out of the 1950 World Cup, had been murdered by Doc's infamous secret police force – the Tonton Macoutes.

The facts of the case were not widely known at the time and Gaetjens' body was never found. Woosnam's only concern, however, was getting the better of the Haitians on the football field when it really mattered. The friendly defeats, and the sole victory, were ultimately meaningless but, if he and his side had learned one thing from their visit, it was that Haiti were a difficult team to beat.

Following his appointment as head coach of the USA, Woosnam did his utmost to instil a sense of excitement in the American people about having a soccer team that was competing on a regular basis. "The response, reaction and emotional involvement of these games are tremendous," he said. "When you play a team from another country, you're not talking about the Mason-Dixon line. You are united as one country in competition with another country. Soccer can provide the public with a sustained emotional experience they may never have previously experienced. Just imagine the atmosphere in a United States stadium filled to the brim with Americans sitting at the edge of their seats watching America play Russia with the score tied 3-3 and five minutes to go. How many of these sports fans are going to leave before the final whistle?"

Woosnam should probably have been worried about whether fans showed up at all. Still not enamoured by the round-ball game, fewer than

3,000 members of the American public turned up for their next World Cup qualifier, when Canada visited the GA Stadium in Atlanta, Georgia, on 27 October. In the fortnight since the sides had last met, Canada had gone to Bermuda and come away with just a point following a 0-0 draw. The islanders, runners-up to Mexico in the 1967 Pan-American Games, were certainly no pushovers at home. Woosnam's team could worry about that later but, in the meantime, they had been presented with a great chance of closing the gap on Canada. They duly did so, with Albrecht hitting the winner for the Americans early in the second half. After four matches, Gerry was still to break his international duck, but the United States' World Cup campaign was finally up and running.

Next up was Bermuda's visit to Kansas, an apt venue given Gerry's subsequent 'There's no place like home' moment. "Bermuda was a British colony and, when we were lined up on the pitch, they started playing *God Save the Queen*. In a moment of sheer instinct, I turned to face the Bermudan flag," he laughs. "The captain nudged me in the ribs and said, 'Gerry, remember you're a fucking American now!'"

That small amount of misplaced loyalty aside, the match turned out to be the high point of Gerry's brief international career. While he is the first to admit that scoring twice against a group of islands with barely 60,000 inhabitants was not quite the same as scoring against Brazil, it nevertheless represented a significant step on the yellow brick road towards World Cup qualification. Peter Millar opened the scoring for the US on 22 minutes, with Gerry doubling the lead shortly afterwards. Bermuda hit back before the break, however, and then equalised shortly after half-time. Gerry restored America's lead before the home side ran out 6-2 winners, Millar completing his hat-trick late on. It was America's biggest ever victory in a competitive match. "Gerry was definitely the protagonist in that game," says Gansler.

Eight days later, on 10 November, the US flew out to Bermuda for the return game at the National Stadium in Hamilton, knowing that only victory would ensure they topped the group and qualified for the semi-finals. Fortunately, the United States succeeded where Canada had failed. An early own goal settled the American nerves, before Roy grabbed a second just before half-time to secure a 2-0 win. The US topped the group, setting up a semi-final with Haiti. If they were to beat the Haitians, however, they would have to do so without the services of Phil Woosnam.

In January 1969, the Welshman quit as head coach of both the US national team and the Atlanta Chiefs, whom he had led to the North American Soccer League championship, to become commissioner of the crisis-hit NASL – a move that would eventually see global stars such as Franz Beckenbauer and Pele playing in a golden, but ultimately unsustainable, period for American soccer. His assistant, Gordon Jago, was placed in charge for the two crunch matches with, hopefully, more to follow. With his employers Coventry in the midst of a second successive relegation battle, Gerry did not feature in the first game on 20 April. Jago cited Gerry's absence as a key reason for the 2-0 defeat in Port-au-Prince, which left the Americans' World Cup dream dangling by a thread.

"He's only a little fellow, but there's a lot of weight on his shoulders to get us through," said Jago ahead of the decider in San Diego on 11 May. If pre-match preparations were anything to go by, however, the manager knew the United States were fighting a losing battle.

"When we arrived at the ground we had three goalkeepers listed in the squad of 22, but we only had two goalkeepers' jerseys," explains Jago. "We had to quickly, and quietly, get the secretary to go to the sports shop in San Diego and buy a third goalkeeper's uniform so that our third goalkeeper didn't feel like a nonentity."

For Gerry, the match itself is a painful memory. "The game was only about 15 minutes old when I got badly injured," he says. "I was tackled and I hit the ground hard. My rib went through my kidney and I was carried off. I came back on and struggled for the rest of the game. Afterwards I was pissing blood. That was the end of my international career and it was probably the biggest disappointment of my entire life. I was desperate for us to qualify for the World Cup and I really believed we could do it."

The match, and the campaign, ended in disappointment for the United States, with Haiti winning 1-0 and qualifying for the final. There they would meet El Salvador, whose own semi-final victory over Honduras famously led to the four-day "Football War".

While America's failure to qualify for the 1970 World Cup was not enough to lead to armed conflict, it was a bitterly disappointing end to Gerry's brief foray into international football. "Gerry was still a good pro and he had good ability but we didn't have the necessary support around him," says Jago. "We didn't have that quality midfielder who would give good service. Gerry and Willy were good players but they didn't have the support to create the openings and the craft that would make it easy for a forward. But Gerry played well and the team did what they could do. They just fell short against Haiti. It would've been nice to have beaten them and gone one or two stages further, but we simply didn't have the quality within the team to be successful at that level. We were a very inexperienced team, but we couldn't have asked for more effort from the players. And, in all honesty, I think we would have struggled immensely had we actually reached the World Cup – I think it was too soon. We'd have had no chance."

Indeed, having made it to the finals, El Salvador failed to score a single goal in Mexico 1970. It would be July 1971 before the United States played another match, and 1990 before they eventually qualified for another World Cup. At the helm during that Italia '90 campaign was Gerry's US team-mate Bob Gansler, who missed the two matches against Haiti through injury.

He says: "The most unfortunate thing about the 1970 qualifying campaign was that, as we were playing our matches, we were getting reports from back home that our league was unravelling (12 NASL teams folded during the season). The psychological impact of things to take the next step was, I think, more than we could handle. Had the league remained intact, had we had something to go to in 1969, I think we would've been there in 1970 as opposed to having to wait until Italia 90. Getting the chance to participate in the ultimate competition in the sport was one of the highlights of my career, as it would be for anybody. If I was asked to be at the World Cup as a player or as a coach I would choose the former, but it was still immense – until Nirvana comes along, that was Nirvana. Italia '90 was the start of a roll for the United States and we've qualified for every World Cup since. Would the US qualifying in 1970 have had the same impact as we had in 1990 and 1994? That's anybody's guess."

On his old team-mate he adds: "Importing pseudo-nationals doesn't always help the team, but Gerry was a plus. I don't think his addition to the squad was anything but positive."

Gerry is philosophical about his time playing under the Star-Spangled Banner. "I was very grateful to be given the chance to play international football and was proud to play for America, I was just disappointed it didn't happen earlier," he says. "We thought that, after we had beaten Bermuda so easily, that we would skate it against Haiti. Maybe we were too confident, I don't know."

Today, Jago describes Gerry as "a pioneer of American soccer", but he wasn't the only Baker striving to take a team into uncharted territory.

18
Zigger-Zagger

It all seemed so fitting. Destiny, perhaps. Ten years after accompanying his older brother to a trial at Stamford Bridge, England international Joe Baker was on the verge of signing for Chelsea. The date was 31 January 1966 and nearly everything was in place. Arsenal had agreed to sell their top goalscorer and Blues manager Tommy Docherty was more than willing to pay the £70,000 transfer fee. "Players of the calibre of Joe Baker only become available once in a lifetime," he gushed.

Joe posed happily with Docherty outside Stamford Bridge and signed autographs for young Chelsea fans. The pair went inside to discuss what was merely the formality of Joe agreeing personal terms. Unfortunately for Chelsea, this was a sticking point. "We cannot agree on terms at all," said Docherty afterwards. "There is no chance of negotiations being resumed."

Joe refused to say whether the disagreement had been over his signing-on fee but it was obvious that, as surely as the deal was seemingly on, it was now most certainly off.

Things hadn't been going well at Arsenal. Since Joe scored his 100th goal for the club in the 5-2 win over Sheffield Wednesday on 28 December 1965, they had lost their first three matches of 1966, with 18-year-old inside right John Radford scoring their only goal of this miserable run in a 2-1 defeat at Blackburn – a team joint-bottom of the league.

When Arsenal returned to Ewood Park for an FA Cup tie a week later and lost 3-0, Billy Wright's patience finally snapped. He immediately dropped two of his star players, George Eastham and Joe, for the next league match against Stoke. The ignominy of being selected to play against Plymouth Argyll Reserves was too much. Both players, who between them had accounted for nearly half of Arsenal's goal tally for the season, immediately handed in transfer requests.

The fact that both were set to be selected in Alf Ramsey's England squad to face West Germany on 23 February was too much for some. Bob Lord, chairman of Burnley, suggested that the Football Association "should support clubs by refusing to pick transfer-seekers for England", adding: "It will be a grave disservice if Mr Ramsey pours glory on Eastham and Baker."

Ramsey chose to ignore Lord's advice and selected both for the squad, although neither played. In fact, Joe and Eastham didn't make their return to first-team action until 8 March. But while Eastham had been able to patch things up with Wright and return to a hero's welcome to face Spurs at Highbury, Joe was making his debut for Nottingham Forest against Burnley.

Forest manager Johnny Carey had spent £65,000 to bring Joe to the City Ground on 26 February, a few days after they had lost 4-0 at home to Leeds. On the face of it, the move didn't seem to be a particularly glamorous one for Joe. Forest were even lower in the league than Arsenal, but the fact they had been prepared to break the club's transfer record to sign him showed that they were ambitious. It was hardly a dream debut for Joe, who hadn't played first-team football for nearly two months. He had also just learned that, while Eastham remained firmly in Alf Ramsey's plans, his own place in the England squad to face the Scottish League had gone to the uncapped John Kaye of West Brom.

Still, a rapturous reception from the Forest fans and a 1-0 victory thanks to a goal from Ian Storey-Moore helped to soften the blow. Four days later, Joe announced his arrival as a Nottingham Forest player with a brace in a 3-3 draw away to Northampton Town. It marked the beginning of a three-and-a-half season love affair with the Reds supporters, who would refer to him as "Zigger Zagger" – a chant borrowed from Chelsea fans – and, mirroring Denis Law's title at Old Trafford, "the King".

"We didn't often get big names at Forest at that stage so Joe was quite a capture," says lifelong Forest fan Richard Williams, chief sports writer at *The Guardian*. "He was a Jimmy Greaves, Michael Owen-type of finisher, but more of a dribbler than Owen. He was very good on the ball and a wonderful goalscorer."

Nevertheless, with Joe scoring only three more goals in a season that culminated in Forest finishing 18th in the table, there was little to suggest that the Reds side of 1966-67 – a team that Williams is proud to be able to reel off from memory – would perform so heroically.

"That side was very well balanced," he explains. "We had Peter Grummitt in goal, one of the best shot-stoppers in the country, and two very strong full-backs in Peter Hindley and John Winfield. Bob McKinlay, who was very experienced and was part of Forest's FA Cup-winning team of 1959, played alongside Terry Hennessey, an excellent player, in the middle of defence. Henry Newton, a local hero, was the John McGovern of the team – not glamorous but essential. Our wingers were Barry Lyons and Ian Storey-Moore, who was very dangerous and scored a lot of goals. Then we had John Barnwell, who was the schemer, Frank Wignall the conventional front man and then Joe Baker, the No 9, who was a finisher. They weren't really a high-scoring team but their build-up play was always very good to watch and Joe Baker was a big part of that."

The legendary Forest side that Storey-Moore describes as "the nearly team" didn't get off to a good start, losing 2-1 at home to Stoke City. It was, however, the fourth season in the last five that Joe had scored on the opening day. Forest then lost away to Chelsea, the club that Joe had come so close to joining, before he and Storey-Moore scored a goal apiece in a 2-1 win at Sheffield United to get Forest's league campaign up and running.

"When Joe came we started to look like we could win things because you could always rely on him to stick his chances away," said Henry Newton. Although results were mixed during the first two months of the season, it was obvious that Joe and Storey-Moore had developed a special understanding. By the end of September, they had scored 11 of Forest's 13 league goals between them.

"We had a great empathy, Joe and I," says Storey-Moore. "I made goals for him and he made goals for me. He was a wonderful player and we had a good working relationship. He arrived at Forest when we were just getting a decent side together. Joe used to get goals out of nothing. You'd go, 'Blimey, how did he do that?'"

Both players were outshone in the next match, when Chris Crowe scored a hat-trick in a memorable 4-1 victory over Manchester United. "The only astonishing thing about that is that Joe didn't score," says Williams.

The result saw Forest leapfrog United in the table, but not for long. They lost 3-0 away to Leicester in their next match and were soundly beaten 4-0 at Anfield a few weeks later. But when Joe scored Forest's first goal in their 3-1 win at home to Sunderland on 12 November, Forest set off on a brilliant run of 13 matches unbeaten, culminating in a 1-0 win over Leeds United on 14 January.

Johnny Carey's side had climbed to third in the table, only a point behind Manchester United and league leaders Liverpool. They stuttered slightly over the next couple of games, drawing against Newcastle and Spurs before finally losing to Manchester United, but Forest were still very much in the hunt for their first ever league championship. They had also managed to negotiate their way through the first two rounds of the FA Cup, with Joe scoring against both Plymouth and Newcastle.

On 18 March, his winner against West Ham at the City Ground kick-started another six-match winning run in the league, taking Forest past Liverpool and into second – still only a point behind Manchester United. Two of the victories in Forest's run had come in successive days against

Burnley. His brace in the 4-1 win at the City Ground, included a goal Richard Williams remembers as the best he saw Joe score for Forest and, according to a Supporters Club article, is "still regarded by many as the most spectacular ever scored by a Forest player".

"I was sitting in the Radcliffe Road end so I had a perfect view," recalls Williams. "Mike Kear crossed the ball in from the right and Joe's overhead kick from the edge of the area flew into the net. It was very spectacular. We then beat Burnley 2-0 at Turf Moor the very next day, with Joe scoring two more."

After taking three attempts to beat Swindon Town, Forest had by this stage reached the last eight of the FA Cup. Supporters were daring to dream that a league and Cup double could be on the cards, but the quarter-final at home to Everton on 8 April would be the last match of the season for one of their star players.

Everton were the FA Cup holders, but Forest had beaten them twice in the league. Joe had scored 19 goals in 39 games since he arrived at the City Ground, including three in the FA Cup but, thanks to Brian Labone, he lasted only two minutes against Everton.

Storey-Moore describes the centre-half's tackle as "rather nasty", while David McVay, author of *Forest's Cult Heroes*, wrote that it "would have stopped a tank in its tracks". Storey-Moore doesn't think the challenge was malicious, but at best it was terribly mistimed. Whatever it was, Joe wouldn't be fit to play for several months. "A lot of us think that that tackle was what lost us the FA Cup," says Williams. "When the first-choice 11 were there, that side functioned beautifully, we could beat anybody, but its weakness was that there was no depth of squad."

Storey-Moore adds: "It really was an horrific injury. I went to see Joe in the treatment room afterwards and his leg was black and blue from top to bottom. He couldn't move it and he didn't play again for the rest of the season. It was a sad loss for him and for Forest. I'm sure we would've won something if it hadn't been for that. We couldn't replace Joe."

Forest lost the FA Cup semi-final to Tottenham and finished runners-up in the league, four points behind champions Manchester United, after winning only three of their last six matches. "It was frustrating that it was such a good team and yet Forest never got any trophies," said Henry Newton.

They had another one at which to aim the following season, when Forest took part in the Inter-Cities Fairs Cup. Joe was no stranger to the competition, having performed so brilliantly against Barcelona for Hibs and scoring Arsenal's first European hat-trick against Staevnet. Now, having recovered from the effects of Labone's tackle with five goals in Forest's first eight league games, he had the chance to help his club to their first victory on the Continent. At this stage Forest, a club now synonymous with the incredible European Cup triumphs of 1979 and 1980 under Brian Clough, had played only two matches in Europe – and lost both.

In 1961-62, they were beaten 7-1 on aggregate by eventual Fairs Cup winners Valencia. Their opponents on 20 September 1967, Eintracht Frankfurt, also had European pedigree, having been European Cup runners-up in 1960. Joe's goal after only 10 minutes in Germany saw him become the first Nottingham Forest player to score in a competitive match on foreign soil. It was also enough to give the club their first victory in European competition. Things got even better in the second leg at the City Ground a month later when Joe, in inspired form, scored twice in the opening 35 minutes to put the tie beyond Frankfurt. Robert Chapman and Barry Lyons also got on the scoresheet in a 4-0 win.

Joe rounded off a good October, from a personal point of view, by scoring in a 1-1 draw at White Hart Lane and grabbing two goals in a 3-1 win at home to Manchester United.

On 31 October, Forest won their third European match in succession with a 2-1 win over FC Zurich, but the away leg a fortnight later saw them come unstuck through the newly introduced away goals rule, with Zurich progressing after a 1-0 win. Forest fans wouldn't get to see their club play in Europe again until the 1978-79 season, but most would agree that it was worth waiting for.

In retrospect, the first-leg victory over Zurich was significant for Joe. It marked the beginning of the longest run of his entire career without a goal – a total of 10 matches. From the moment he burst on to the scene as a 17-year-old at Hibs, through his frustrations in the super-defensive top-flight in Italy and on to the free-scoring Arsenal, Joe Baker had scored goals, and plenty of them.

In fairness, the entire Forest team was struggling, scoring only four times in the seven league matches following the win over Manchester United. When Joe finally found the net again, in a 3-1 win at Stoke on 30 December, the club's new record signing scored his first goal for Forest.

The club had splashed out £100,000 to bring former Rangers great Jim Baxter to the City Ground from Sunderland. Now 28, the Scotsman had become most famous to non-Rangers fans for playing keepie-uppie against England earlier in the year, in the 3-2 victory that saw Scotland supporters crowning their side "unofficial world champions".

Baxter could be brilliant, but he brought with him a hard-drinking reputation that Richard Williams says was the beginning of the end for his favourite Forest side. "The signing of Jim Baxter – that really destroyed the team," he says. "He was unquestionably a great player, but after one marvellous performance for Sunderland against Forest the chairman bought him without consulting Johnny Carey. To introduce a prima donna with dodgy habits into the dressing room was ruinous. His way of life affected the dressing room and he took young players with him. Carey was quiet and not an assertive man. It was a catastrophe – any Forest fan will tell you that."

The 1966-67 runners-up finished 11th in the league, not helped by the fact that Storey-Moore had to spend a considerable amount of time on the sidelines and that Joe's striking partner, Frank Wignall, had been sold to Wolves in February.

But despite his lean spells, Joe scored 21 goals during the season – his best return since joining Forest. Even then, Storey-Moore, whose own career was ended by injury at the age of 28, believes the writing was on the wall.

"I didn't think Joe was ever quite the same after his injury against Everton," he says. "He did well to come back and he scored a few goals the following season, but I'm sure that injury ultimately affected his career. He lost that bit of pace which took him away from defenders and enabled him to score those spectacular goals."

The following season, 1968-69, turned out to be Joe's last during what he described as a "wonderfully happy" spell in Nottingham. The Forest fans had taken "Zigger Zagger" to their hearts and, in return, he had given them memories that they would treasure forever. It was just a shame that the Joe Baker who left Nottingham was not the same player who had arrived three years earlier. By the beginning of December 1968, Forest were second bottom of the league. They had won just one of their 19 matches, with Joe having scored only three times in the 13 games in which he had featured. Manager Johnny Carey was sacked and replaced by Matt Gillies, the Scotsman who had spent the last ten years at Leicester. Unfortunately, he wasn't able to prevent Forest from crashing spectacularly at the first hurdle of the FA Cup, losing 3-0 at Preston North End.

Although his reign at Forest ended in 1972 following the disappointment of relegation, Gillies did sign future European Cup heroes Martin O'Neill and John Robertson, who cleaned Joe's boots as a 15-year-old apprentice.

"I was just a kid so unfortunately I didn't get to play alongside Joe, but I played against him in practice matches," says Robertson. "He was like shit off a shovel. His movement was fantastic and he could always get a goal. I used to clean his boots, but it was a privilege to be at the same club. Joe is an absolute legend in the city of Nottingham. Everybody talked about him and everyone remembers Joe Baker."

Indeed, in his 1991 book, *Nottingham Forest – A Complete Record*, author Pete Attaway writes: "Of all the players to appear for Nottingham Forest over the years, possibly only the current skipper, Stuart Pearce, could rival Joe Baker in popularity."

This much was obvious when Joe returned to a hero's welcome at the City Ground in 1995. The feeling of affection was mutual. In an article entitled *Return of a Legend* in the *Nottingham Evening Post*, Joe said: "I loved it at Forest. They were the best club side I played for. But what has always hurt me is that we never fulfilled our potential. From being the 'nearly, nearly' men of 1966-67 we should have gone on to win trophies. The City Ground was packed like sardines in my time and they gave us deafening support."

Storey-Moore, who spent two seasons at Manchester United after leaving Forest, says: "If Joe had been playing now he would've been on £150,000 a week, at a top club and a superstar. We finished second in the league, nearly won our first ever championship, and he was an integral part of that. He was top drawer – one of the best centre-forwards I've ever seen."

Sadly, by the end of season 1968-69, with Forest finishing 18th in the league, it was clear that Joe's best playing days were behind him. A total of 31 appearances, including one in the League Cup, had yielded only four goals. They were the kind of figures that nobody, not least the man himself, would ever associate with Joe Baker. But perhaps it could be put down as a blip – one bad season among numerous prolific ones. At the age of only 28, he felt he had a lot more to give. At the very least, Joe figured that things couldn't get worse. He was wrong.

19
Mackem Misery

Dennis Tueart often finds himself in demand from journalists. The former England international is amiable, approachable and always happy to help, yet he can't help but notice that it's the same two questions that always crop up: 'How did it feel to score one of the greatest goals in the history of the League Cup?' And 'How did it feel to be the man who replaced Pele?'

It's probably something of a relief, then, that the former Manchester City and New York Cosmos star is asked to remember a different time in his career, when he was asked to take the place of another legendary goalscorer.

"One of my real breakthrough moments came on 19 September 1970," recalls the former Sunderland winger, who was a teenager when Joe Baker arrived at Roker Park in the summer of '69. "We were playing Sheffield Wednesday at home and, just after half-time, I came on as a substitute to replace Joe. I made one goal and scored another and we won 3-1. I was only 19. We were like kings at home and I got fantastic exposure because of that game."

For teenager Tueart, it was a watershed. For Joe, the incident was another reminder that he was now 30 years old and, for the first time in his 13-year career, he was now plying his trade in the second tier.

When Alan Brown, in his second spell as Sunderland manager, brought Joe to Wearside for £30,000 in July 1969, Neil Armstrong and Buzz Aldrin had just landed on the moon, but the Black Cats had been struggling to lift off from the bottom end of the table since they had won promotion to the First Division in 1964.

They had recently sold 20-year-old Colin Suggett to West Brom for £100,000. Suggett had scored nine league goals the previous season, a decent record in a struggling side, and Joe, who had once scored that many in a single game, felt he was up to the task. "We had a very young team and we were going through a particularly sticky period," recalls Tueart. "Alan Brown was an innovative coach and he brought in three experienced players: Gordon Harris, Calvin Palmer and Joe Baker to balance things up a bit."

From a personal point of view, there was good news for Joe, Sonia and young Nadia, as they welcomed Colin Baker into the world on 14 July.

Like Nadia, Colin was born in Scotland, somewhere where the family would spend a great deal of time during Joe's stint on Wearside.

"When we were in Sunderland – near enough to come home in three hours – we spent every weekend here (Scotland), and it completely unsettled me," said Sonia. "I just wanted to come home again – and so did Joe. So we decided to go house-hunting – with the idea that I could live here permanently, and he could travel up at weekends, or whenever he had free time. We made a lot of friends, particularly in Nottingham, where I really loved it. So much so, that when Joe was moved to Sunderland – I was against the place before I ever saw it. I didn't really settle there – in fact I never watched a game, and that's most unusual for me. I'm a regular spectator."

That was probably no bad thing. Sunderland were a young team, but there was a familiar figure in Gordon Harris, who had gained his one and only England cap during the 1-1 draw against Poland in January 1966 – Joe's final appearance for the national side.

Eyeing a place in the World Cup squad must have seemed like a very distant memory when Sunderland kicked off their new league campaign at Coventry City. Joe's older brother didn't make it on to the pitch, and now Joe, too, wished he was elsewhere.

"I should have found out before I signed that Alan Brown played with nine men back and one up front," he said later. "In the first game nobody else was allowed over the halfway line. I knew then that I'd made a mistake."

After eight league games, Sunderland already looked like odds-on favourites for relegation, having lost six, drawn two and having scored only four goals. Even when Sunderland did finally register a win on 20 September, against fellow strugglers Nottingham Forest, Joe wasn't among the scorers against his former club. And Joe could have done with the assistance of FIFA's infamous "dodgy goals committee" in the following match against Spurs when, for the only time in the season, Sunderland recorded back-to-back wins. Joe challenged for a high ball with Mike England and Peter Collins and, as recalled by Jimmy Greaves in his autobiography: "Somehow the ball became wedged between all three bodies before squirting out and past Pat Jennings. The referee was in a quandary as to who had actually applied the final touch. No one was sure, though of course Joe Baker was adamant that it had been him. In the end, the referee put it down as a Mike England own goal. Not that it mattered to us."

But it mattered to Joe. When his miserable scoreless run had stretched to 18 league matches, and Sunderland were propping up the table with only 10 points, *The Sun* ran an article about Joe under the headline "When the goals won't come". One of British football's deadliest marksmen now cut a very lonely figure as he wrote his name in the sand at Roker Beach. It was now mid-November and Joe had scored a solitary goal in the whole of 1969 – at the beginning of March. "I'd never felt so miserable," he said. "I seemed to be on my own up front. I was taking all the 'treatment' from defenders and getting no support."

For Joe, the decade had started in such spectacular fashion, with him striking fear into the hearts of Barcelona, Juventus and Roma. Now, he was unable to find the net against Bradford and Burnley.

"Joe became a fan favourite even though he didn't get the goals everybody thought he would," says former Sunderland goalkeeper Jim Montgomery, the club's record appearance maker. "They knew it wasn't for want of trying. If he wasn't trying then they would suss that out, but Joe always gave 100 per cent in every game. We thought he'd be a great addition to the squad as he was a big name, but we were a very young side and we struggled, especially in the First Division. We brought him in to get the goals but that took a while to happen. At his previous clubs, he had great players to supply chances for him, but he came into a Sunderland team that wasn't very good. The opportunities didn't come too readily for him."

Gerry, whose own top-flight career was rapidly coming to an end, says: "At Roker Park was the only time in Joe's career that he was disappointed with himself. I don't know why. I suppose you need a team around you and they weren't very good."

Echoing Ian Storey-Moore, Tueart says: "One of Joe's main assets was his sharpness. He used to be so quick that it was frightening. He had absolutely explosive pace. I think, by the time he came to Sunderland, that sharpness and that pace had started to wane a bit. He wasn't frightened of hard work in training but he had just lost that little yard of pace. But maybe the team around him weren't good at supplying what he deserved, because in the box he was still explosive. As a club, we were struggling desperately. That balance of experience and youth that Alan Brown was aiming for didn't quite work."

After a 2-0 defeat to Leeds on 19 November, Joe didn't feature again until 27 December, when he finally got on the scoresheet with the equaliser in a 1-1 draw at home to Manchester United. "Joe was still lethal in and around the box, you could see that every day in training," says Montgomery.

On the training pitch was also where Joe – in his own unique style – was able to give the young members of the Sunderland squad the benefit of his experience.

"He always used to take the mick out of me," laughs Tueart. "I was a left winger at the time but I was right-footed and his mickey-taking used to spur me on to become better with my left foot. He used to give me so much stick about it so, in training, Gordon Harris would hit the ball out to me on the wing and I would cross with my weaker left foot to Joe in the middle, just so I could get better. And it worked. Joe made me realise that you can't just sit on your backside. You've got to work hard at everything. He had a great sense of humour. He would take the mick and he was one of the leading banter merchants in the dressing room. While we were all young and up and coming, he had been there, done it and bought the T-shirt. It was fantastic for me to play and to train with Joe because he had an amazing instinct to score goals. His movement was excellent."

But despite his excellence in training, Joe featured in only five more matches in the 1969-70 season, scoring once more in the 3-1 defeat to Chelsea at Stamford Bridge. "We had some outstanding young players – Bobby Kerr, Ian Porterfield, Billy Hughes, Dennis Tueart – but the manager stifled them," said Joe later. "He held back their development. He put reins on them."

Although it had for so long seemed an inevitability, Sunderland were relegated only by a single point. Joe got back among the goals against German opposition during pre-season, scoring in the 2-1 victory over Eintracht Brunswick and then getting a hat-trick in the 4-3 win over Hannover 96. Life in the old English Second Division began with a bittersweet experience. Sunderland lost 4-3 away to Bristol City, but Joe scored twice in a competitive match for the first time in nearly two and a half years. And two weeks later, when Sunderland marked their first win of the season with a 3-0 victory over Charlton at Roker Park, he celebrated his first competitive hat-trick since November 1963.

Joe was finding goals a lot easier to come by in the Second Division and scored three in two games at the beginning of December, taking his season's tally to 10. But his equaliser in the 3-1 defeat away to Cardiff on 12 December turned out to be his last goal in English football.

That month, Alan Brown paid Rotherham £100,000 for the services of Dave Watson, a big striker who, following a hugely successful conversion to centre half, would become an England regular for nearly a decade. Joe was delighted by Watson's arrival, believing a big front man would be the perfect foil, but Brown immediately handed Joe's No.9 shirt to his new signing.

"I was overjoyed when Dave Watson came," recalled Joe. "I thought, 'Great, we've got a big man for me to feed off, like Geoff Strong at Arsenal and Frank Wignall at Forest.' The next thing I knew I was on the touchline. The manager wasn't thinking right. Dave Watson was just the sort of player for me to play off and get the best out of me."

Joe spent the next three league matches on the bench, only being re-called to the side to face Leyton Orient in the FA Cup on 11 January because Watson was Cup-tied. Sunderland lost the match 3-0. Two years later, Second Division Sunderland would win the FA Cup in one of the biggest upsets in the history of the competition. By that time, Alan Brown had gone and been replaced by local hero Bob Stokoe.

Jim Montgomery, whose brilliant double save was credited as one of the main reasons Sunderland beat Leeds at Wembley, says that, although Joe had difficulty finding the net at Roker Park, he still played a valuable role on Wearside. "He was a lovely lad and he got on tremendously well with everyone at the club," he says. "The younger lads all looked up to him."

Tueart adds: "The majority of the young footballers Joe played with at Sunderland matured into the side that won the FA Cup."

But there was to be no silverware for Joe. Four days after the FA Cup defeat to Orient, he was playing for another club – one whose fans had been crying out for his return.

20
Second Coming

By early 1971, Aberdeen were on a roll. Eddie Turnbull had guided his side to the top of the old Scottish First Division after winning 15 matches in a row – a run stretching back three and a half months. Even more remarkably, the club hadn't conceded a goal in the last 12 games, with goalkeeper Bobby Clark setting a new Scottish record after keeping more than 1,000 hours' worth of clean sheets.

Next up for the league leaders was a visit to Easter Road, with Turnbull's visit to the ground where he was worshipped as a player fully expected to result in another win and, more than likely, another clean sheet for Aberdeen.

It would take something special to stop the Dons in their tracks. Fortunately for Hibs, that something special had arrived. He looked a little older, he wore white boots and he sported an impressive pair of mutton chops, but there was no mistaking Joe Baker.

"It was like the messiah returning," recalls former Hibs forward Kenny Davidson, who was only 18 when Joe made his return to Scottish football on 16 January 1971. "He was a legend at Easter Road and the news that he was coming back lifted the club and the supporters were full of expectation."

The crowd of 23,000 was more than Hibs' previous three home matches put together, with few able to comprehend that the legendary striker had returned to the place where he first made his name. But his £12,000 move almost didn't happen. Disappointed at the way his career at Sunderland had been going, Joe's mother Lizzie had intimated that he should contemplate calling it a day.

"I was more or less convinced I'd had it," admitted Joe. "Then, just when I was on the point of asking Sunderland to cancel my contract, bang, everything seemed to happen at once."

St Mirren manager Wilson Humphries had driven to Roker Park to persuade Joe to follow in his older brother's footsteps and come to Paisley. While considering the offer of going to Love Street, Sunderland manager Alan Brown rang Joe to say that Hibs boss Dave Ewing, who won the FA Cup as a player with Manchester City in 1956, also wanted his signature.

"No further discussion was required," said Joe. "I jumped at the chance to re-join them. The only drawback was that people might expect to see the same Joe Baker they saw playing 10 years ago."

In order to accommodate Joe for his debut against Aberdeen, Ewing dropped Jim Blair to the bench and even made his new signing captain for the day. But Joe Baker hadn't returned to Easter Road to make a novelty cameo for the sake of lifting the club's spirits. He was there to score goals and, following a goalless first half, he gave his adoring public exactly what they wanted. Four minutes after Pat Stanton had fired past Bobby Clark to end the goalkeeper's record of consecutive clean sheets, Joe headed home his first goal in Scotland for nearly a decade.

"I had gone from watching him in the stands to playing alongside him," says Jimmy O'Rourke, who admits he hero-worshipped Joe as a youngster. "I was trying to think who I could compare him to, but I couldn't think of anyone – except maybe Roy of the Rovers."

Hibs won the watch 2-1, their first victory in 10 matches, they had beaten the mighty Aberdeen and a hero from yesteryear had scored the winning goal on his return to the club he played for as a teenager. Even the men behind Roy Race's larger-than-life exploits would have struggled to concoct such a compelling storyline.

"The players were in awe of Joe," says Stanton. "When he ran out on to the park he was wearing white boots, which I couldn't remember any players in Scotland wearing at the time, but he showed that he could still play. A lot of players rely on speed and, when it goes, they've not got the technique. Everybody gets old and Joe had been away from Easter Road for a while but he was still very quick and, allied to his experience, he knew when to use that pace. He didn't rely 100 per cent on his speed."

But it wasn't just on the pitch that Joe proved an invaluable presence in the Hibs ranks. "When you're young you've got your heroes and Joe was the player you admired most," says Stanton, who watched Joe from the terracing as a 13-year-old.

"He was tremendous, so dynamic. He was strong, he was quick, he was brave and he was a really good-looking guy as well. He had everything. Years later, when I eventually got to meet him, I found that he was a nice man as well. He knew he was a good player but he didn't blow his own trumpet. Sometimes you find your heroes can be a let-down when you meet them in person because you've had them placed on a pedestal for so long, but that was never the case with Joe. When he came back to Hibs he was full of advice and he went out of his way to help you. You could learn a lot from him, especially that you had to work very hard. You would make mistakes but he said that was just you learning. He would take you aside and have a wee word with you and invariably he was right."

Not always, as Joe showed in his next match when he was sent off for a challenge on Ian Munro in the 3-1 defeat to St Mirren. It was the first time Joe had been given his marching orders in senior Scottish football but he made up for it in the next match when he scored in a 1-0 win over Motherwell.

Thoughts of Joe's four-goal heroics of 1958 sprang to mind when Hibs came up against city rivals Hearts in the fourth round of the Scottish Cup at Tynecastle. Although he didn't score in the 2-1 win, Joe had the distinction of being the only player to feature in both of Hibs' Cup victories at Tynecastle since 1910.

Back in the league, Joe scored in the 1-1 draw against Rangers at Ibrox and, in Hibs' first Scottish Cup quarter-final since 1965, gave his side the chance to set up another meeting with Rangers when he was tripped in the area by Dundee's George Stewart. O'Rourke dispatched the spot-kick in the bad-tempered match which saw 20 fans arrested, but Hibs kept alive their hopes of a first Scottish Cup victory in 69 years – and ensured that Joe's fairy tale comeback continued.

"If you'd told me then that I'd be back playing centre-forward for Hibs and enjoying my football into the bargain, I would have thought you were off your rocker," he said.

"I still prefer to lead the line from the front, and Hibs' present style of keeping the wingers wide gives me greater scope in the middle. It makes such a difference when you have a choice of forwards to pass the ball to. In most cases I don't need to take time to control the ball – I know there are several players ready to come through. It's just a case of heading the ball on to them first time. What a pleasant change from English football where everything is so tight at the back."

It was certainly a vast improvement on his days at Roker Park. Although he had only re-joined Hibs in January, Joe's record of eight goals in 11 league matches since his return made him the club's top league scorer – two ahead of O'Rourke. And though Hibs lost the Cup semi-final to Rangers following a replay, Joe was thrilled with his return to Scottish football.

"It's been like starting all over again," he said. "Just like the old days, being constantly mobbed at the ground. But they can chase me all they like. It's when the youngsters stop caring I'll begin to worry – like at Sunderland. The way I'm feeling right now, it'll be some time before I get a repeat of the 'pack it in' blues."

This was in sharp contrast to Dave Ewing who, following Hibs' 12th-place finish in the league, called time on his brief managerial career. His successor was a popular choice among Hibs supporters, as Eddie Turnbull, who had won the Scottish Cup with Aberdeen during his six years at Pittodrie, returned to Easter Road.

Already a legend as a player, the notoriously strict Turnbull would come to be revered as a manager, with "Turnbull's Tornadoes" winning the League Cup in 1973 and finishing runners-up in the championship the following season. Joe began life under the command of his former team-mate in promising fashion, scoring in three successive matches in the League Cup before picking up a hip injury against Motherwell that would blight his season.

He was out of action for six weeks, appearing in five league games in October and November. Before conceding that he would have to undergo surgery, Joe scored in the 3-2 win over Kilmarnock on 27 November. Joe didn't play again until 19 February, and it was only thanks to the heavy tackling of Alex Ferguson that he saw a return to action against Falkirk.

Alex Cropley, a skilful winger, was forced to limp off after breaking his ankle in a challenge by the future Manchester United manager, and Joe, coming off the bench, celebrated his return to action by setting up a goal for Alan Gordon and then scoring with a spectacular diving header to secure Hibs' first league win in over a month.

It was ironic that Joe found himself replacing Cropley. Five months earlier, the Aldershot-born youngster had made his Scotland debut against Portugal alongside Joe's former Arsenal team-mate Bob Wilson, who was born in Chesterfield. Together, they were the first English-born players to turn out for Scotland under a rule change that, had it come into effect a decade or so earlier, might have had considerable significance for the Scottish national team.

"Imagine Joe Baker and Denis Law playing up front for Scotland," says Jimmy O'Rourke. "We'd have won the World Cup!" This was now, sadly, out of the question, but Hibs finally recapturing the Scottish Cup remained a possibility, especially when Joe scored in successive 2-0 victories over Airdrie in round four and in the quarter-finals against Turnbull's former club Aberdeen.

For the second season in a row, Hibs were drawn against Rangers in the semi-finals. After Joe scored in the 3-0 win over Partick Thistle, Hibs played St Johnstone at Easter Road. The match, played on 8 April, turned into a rout – a 7-1 win for Hibs marking their biggest league victory for six years. But the match was significant for another reason. It marked the last of Joe Baker's 158 goals in a green and white shirt.

A week later, Joe lined up against Rangers in front of 76,000 spectators at Hampden Park. After trailing to Alex McDonald's opener, Joe played a part in Hibs' equaliser when his shot was parried by Peter McCloy and into the path of O'Rourke, whose goal took the tie to a replay. Sadly for Joe, it was a match in which he would play no part. For the next league fixture against Dundee, he was dropped in favour of John Hazel – a player who was only four years old when Joe made his Hibs debut back in 1957.

It was a sobering thought for Joe who, now aged 32, found himself deep in "veteran" territory. He watched from the bench as Hibs did what they had failed to do the previous season and dispatched Rangers 2-0 in the replay to reach their first Scottish Cup final since Joe had lined up alongside the likes of Tom Preston and John Fraser in 1958.

And on 28 April 1972, just over a week before the big match at Hampden, Joe was released from his contract. "Joe had been carrying a couple of injuries that, at his age, were just enough to hold him back a wee bit," says Stanton. "He had been in the game a long time and he was realistic enough to know that was the situation. A time comes when you realise that you've had your day in the sun and you've got to move on."

But Joe hadn't enjoyed his last day in the sun. Not yet.

21
What Now?

"When you have been used to the big time and the headlines, it isn't easy to sit down and accept that it's over." Joe Baker's musings on retirement from the professional game will sound familiar, especially to those footballers who played in an era when becoming a multi-millionaire by the age of 21 was fantasy, as opposed to standard contract conditions. Neither of the Baker brothers was keen to end their playing careers, but both were conscious that they needed to have one eye on the future.

Having made a solitary, substituted, appearance for the club during the 1969-70 season and having spent three months on loan at Fourth Division Brentford, Gerry was released by Coventry City in the summer of 1970. "I absolutely loved my time at Coventry, but the more times you read the newspapers describing you as a veteran, the more you believe it," he says.

He began his brief foray into management on the south coast with non-league Margate, taking over from former Spurs striker Almer Hall, who had held the position since 1950. Still only 33 and having played in a World Cup qualifier only a year previously, Gerry joined as player-manager and, despite missing a number of games through injury, finished as the club's joint top-scorer with 11 goals in his first season.

While he still had what it took to put the ball in the net, however, Gerry felt he was "too soft" to cut it as a manager. He left the club 11 games into the next season.

Gerry's affinity with Coventry continued as he settled down for a long career at the Jaguar car plant, while continuing to play non-league football with Nuneaton Borough, Bedworth United and Worcester City before finally hanging up his boots at the age of 37.

Joe, too, was in no hurry to call time on his playing days. After he was released by Hibs, former Scotland goalkeeper George Farm signed him for Second Division Raith Rovers. Joe's first season at Stark's Park yielded 25 goals in 24 league matches, and he pleased supporters of both persuasions in his second when he scored against Hibs in a League Cup defeat at Easter Road.

After scoring 43 goals in 66 games in two seasons at the Kirkcaldy club, Joe failed to agree terms with Farm to stay on for a third season. Nor was he interested in prolonging his career by dropping into midfield or defence. "I wanted to go out as a striker – I had never played anything else and didn't want to," he said.

Joe played his last game in senior football with a 60-minute appearance at Stark's Park on 7 August 1974, during a pre-season friendly against Preston North End. The opposition seemed appropriate, given that the English Third Division side were being managed by Bobby Charlton. Joe's former international colleague scored the last of Preston's goals in a 4-0 win. Having overseen Preston's drop to the third tier of English football, Charlton was soon forced to concede that he wasn't cut out for management. Although keen to stay in the game, Joe found that more and more of his time was being spent at The Central Bar in Craigneuk, the pub not far from his Wishaw home that he had taken over shortly after signing for Raith.

He had already tried his hand at operating his "Top of the League" ice cream vans while still at Hibs, but felt there was more money to be made in the pub game. It was a common profession among former footballers but not, he quickly learned, the easiest way to earn a living. "After a couple of years of pulling pints and stopping punch-ups, I had to get out or risk losing my sanity," he said later. "To be frank, not too many of my customers were easy-going punters who enjoyed a couple of drinks and a laugh. More a bucketful and an argument."

After Joe had sold the pub, Gerry helped him get a job at British Leyland's truck plant in Bathgate. Like just about any other occupation he could have imagined, working on the production line and, later, on a building site, was a big improvement on running the pub but, as a former international footballer, he felt he had plenty to give back to the game he loved. "I should have stayed on and given the benefit of my experience to the kids coming through," he said, adding, "I feel I have a lot to offer football and would dearly love to manage a senior side."

Having seen players such as Charlton walk into managerial positions in England, Joe found his own situation increasingly frustrating. "Perhaps I wore the wrong colours at international level," he fumed. "I was categorised as English, which is nonsense since I'm Scottish through and through and would dearly love to have worn the dark blue jersey. But the Scottish press at the time had me down for being English and it wasn't unusual for me to score something like 10 goals in five games for Arsenal or Nottingham Forest without getting a mention in the papers up here. As a result, I was something of a forgotten man in Scotland, and maybe this is partly responsible for me failing to land a managerial or coaching job here. I've applied for many positions but I've consistently been told that I have no track record. That's a joke. After all, I could name a lot of current managers in Scotland who, as players, lived in the insular world of one club and still walked into jobs. If I were playing now I would be a millionaire."

After gaining his coaching badges at Largs and gaining experience at Junior sides Fauldhouse United and Blantyre Celtic, Joe was finally given his chance to enter senior management in May 1981, at the age of 40, when he successfully applied to take over at Second Division (then the bottom tier of Scottish football) Albion Rovers.

He found himself in an impossible situation with the struggling part-timers, however, and his tenure lasted only until December following a 6-1 defeat at Berwick Rangers. "I was coach, manager, sponge man and trainer," he said of the match at Shielfield Park. "I only had 11 fit players. One of the substitutes had a bad knee, the other a pulled hamstring . . . The inevitable happened. One of our boys got a bad leg gash after ten minutes. Blood everywhere, and I'm on the park sponging away. I shouted to the first sub to get warmed up. 'I cannae, I cannae run' he shouted back. I told him to walk up and down the line. Their physio came on to help and I took the injured lad off, then told the first sub to stand out on the right wing. I had just returned from the tunnel when the second sub tells me the goalkeeper has been done. Right, you're on, I said, at least you won't need to run. I thought Frank Connor, who was Berwick's manager, was going to collapse with laughter in the other dug-out."

Staying on in an assistant capacity, Joe was again given the chance to take the reins in 1984, with Rovers having finished bottom of the league the previous season. By the end of the 1984-85 season, Joe had guided them to a reasonably respectable ninth – an improvement of five places on the previous campaign. He stayed in the position until December 1985, by which time a series of crushing results and only two league wins brought an end to his managerial career for good.

Scottish sports journalist Graham Spiers suggested that Joe was "too gentle, too caring" for the role, adding that he was "the type who skips around behind a player for a quiet word in his ear".

Like his former England team-mate Johnny Haynes, Joe won nothing as a player, but he finally got his hands on silverware in 1989 when, as assistant to former Rangers and Scotland defender Davie Provan, Albion were crowned Second Division champions. "This is the best thing that's ever happened to me in football," Joe said while clutching the trophy. "It means more than anything I did as a player. These lads have full-time jobs.

They come home from work and go straight out to train in the cold and dark. It's a tremendous achievement for them."

But the following year, another club cried out for Joe's help, one that held a particularly special place in his heart, and he wasn't about to refuse.

22
Lost Fairway

Sometimes, actions speak louder than words. It was the summer of 1990 and the very existence of the club that both Joe and Gerry Baker had represented with such distinction was under threat.

Wallace Mercer, the chairman of Hearts, had suggested that the only way to challenge the dominance of Glasgow's Old Firm was for his club to merge with their great Edinburgh rivals – Hibs – and create an "Edinburgh United", to be based on the outskirts of the city. Rather than a merger, however, many supporters in the east of Scotland's capital saw the proposal as a takeover. Either way, if Mercer succeeded in his plans, Hibernian Football Club would be no more.

Although a number of impassioned speeches and pleas were made during the six-week "Hands off Hibs" campaign, it was one simple, wordless, act that sticks in the minds of supporters. Joe Baker, who had thrilled a generation of fans with his extraordinary exploits in front of goal, got down on his knees and kissed the Easter Road turf. The crowd erupted, the tears flowed and, ultimately, the campaign to save Hibs was won.

"Joe was a god at Easter Road," says good friend Willie McEwan, chairman of the Hibs Former Players Association. "He didn't want anyone to take the club – his club – away from the supporters. It was like the Pope stepping off an aircraft and kissing the tarmac. That one action epitomised the strength of feeling against the merger. With Joe, everything came from the heart. He was never a businessman. He was a man who had real feelings and belief in what he did."

Such was the esteem in which Joe was held at Hibs that he was given a new role on match days, entertaining guests in the hospitality lounge with stories from his colourful career. The one about the teenage English footballer and the London taxi driver always proved popular.

Even though Joe's footballing career, much like his brother's, was nomadic ("I've got a wardrobe full of ties because I played for so many clubs!" says Gerry), adulation for the striker wasn't the sole preserve of football fans in Edinburgh.

An emotional visit to Nottingham Forest's City Ground in 1989 was greeted with "Return of the King" headlines and a series of letters from misty-eyed supporters to the *Evening Post*. And despite being in Italy only a year, the crowd roared its approval in 2001 when Joe, wearing a brand new "Baker 9" claret shirt, waved to supporters at his old stomping ground in Torino. "I have a feeling of gratitude towards Joe Baker for the joy he gave me when I was a young Torino supporter," said the club's president, Attilio Romero.

And then there is north London. "I remember going to a quiz and one of the teams was called the Joe Baker Appreciation Society," laughs former Arsenal team-mate David Court. "The last time I saw him was when he visited the old Highbury. He was a little worse for wear because everybody wanted to buy him a drink."

This kind of affection for the Baker Boy made the events of Monday, 6 October 2003 all the more difficult to bear. Preparing to tee-off at Lanark Golf Club, former Celtic striker John "Dixie" Deans removes one of his most prized possessions, a driver, from his bag. "Joe gave it to me the week before he died," he says. "It's a difficult club to use, but Joe could certainly use it."

It was on this course that Joe, playing in a charity golf tournament alongside Deans and a number of other celebrities, suffered a heart attack. He was rushed to Wishaw General Hospital, but died shortly afterwards. "It was a terrible day," says Deans. "I was playing in the group behind Joe and all of a sudden there was panic. He was the nicest man you could ever meet. I'm from Paisley and I've been a St Mirren supporter all my life. Gerry was my idol and I always said to Joe that I wanted to meet him. The two of them were the best of pals and Joe said that I would get to meet him. I did – but it was at Joe's funeral." Following Joe's death, Fraser Wishart, now chief executive of the Professional Footballers' Association Scotland, said: "Joe had been working to help former players by being very active in the formation of a former players' association and former players' benevolent fund. You could not meet a nicer, more genuine man and his death will be felt very hard here."

Joe's children, Nadia and Colin, admit that their mother was "never the same" after their father's death. Sonia died in 2010. Anne Baker, who passed away in 2012, described the effect Joe's death had on her husband: "It was like cutting off his right arm."

"I still miss him," says Gerry. "It was bloody awful. We were like twins."

Colin says: "If Nadia or I ever had any problems, he was the man who could fix it. There was a period when we didn't get to see him very much when we were kids because he was so busy with the pub but, years later, we got really close and I used to sit in the living room with him and we'd chat for hours. I'm so grateful I got to spend that time with him. He was so proud of us and we were so proud of him."

Colin looks over at his six-year-old twin sons, Callum and Joseph, as they play happily with their sister, Ellie, in the family living room. Both boys are wearing Arsenal shirts with "Baker 9" on the back.

"They're both brilliant at football," smiles Colin. "My dad used to tell me that he couldn't wait to have grandkids. It's such a shame that he never had that pleasure. It's only now that I really begin to appreciate how good he was. I've still got so many questions I'd like to ask him. I know he was an England international, a hero at Hibs, Torino, Arsenal, Nottingham Forest . . . but to me and Nadia he was just Dad."

Epilogue
End of the Line

Damnation, must this train be quite so busy? Somewhat vexed, the smartly dressed man with the receding hair and the briefcase makes his way along the corridor, peering into one compartment followed by another as he searches for an empty seat.

Eventually, he finds what he's looking for. He opens the door to the compartment, goes inside and sits down. He opens his briefcase, takes out his newspaper and begins to read. He could be any other commuter on the London to Ipswich line, returning home from another hard day at the office. But a young man in one of the other compartments has recognised him.

The sight of the smartly dressed man with the receding hair and the briefcase has given Gerry Baker a dilemma. Should he sit here with his Ipswich Town team-mates or should he seize this rare opportunity, one that might never come again?

Gerry fidgets in his seat, indecisive. After a few minutes, the train gets under way. He and his friends resume their conversation. They talk about the match, they share a joke but, all the while, Gerry can't stop thinking about the man who has just boarded the train.

Time passes. He looks out of the window. Ipswich is approaching. It won't be long now. He must be decisive. Speak now or forever hold his peace.

'Sod it,' he thinks. He makes his excuses, stands up and steps out into the corridor. He walks slowly, casually. He looks into one compartment, then the next, thinking about what he might say.

Then he spots him. Even with his head buried in a newspaper, the pose is unmistakable. Gerry takes a deep breath and opens the door.

"Excuse me," he says in his familiar west of Scotland drawl. "Mr Ramsey? Do you have a moment?"

Alf Ramsey, the manager of the England national football team, the man who has vowed to bring glory to his country when the 1966 World Cup kicks off in a few months' time, peers over the top of his newspaper. A flash of recognition crosses his stern features. He puts down his reading material and gestures with his hand to the empty seat opposite. Gerry accepts the silent offer and sits down.

Ramsey speaks, a clipped English accent that is now familiar to millions. "What can I do for you, Mr Baker?"

"Erm . . ."

Gerry Baker, a young man renowned for saying exactly what he thinks, is suddenly lost for words. Ramsey's dark eyebrows furrow. He looks impatient. If Mr Baker has nothing to say then he would be as well to say nothing elsewhere and let him read his newspaper in peace.

"Well, Mr Ramsey, it's about my brother . . ."

Ramsey keeps his gaze on Gerry, his eyes urging him to continue.

"I know it's not really my place but, well, I was just wondering, if . . ."

"Well?"

Gerry takes a deep breath and goes for broke.

"I just wanted to know, Mr Ramsey, whether you're planning to put my brother, Joe, in your squad for the World Cup."

Ramsey says nothing. No sense stopping now, thinks Gerry. "It's just that, well, I think he deserves to be in the squad. He could help you win the World Cup, Mr Ramsey. I think he's the best."

The England manager raises a quizzical eyebrow. "Oh, you think so, do you?"

"Well, Mr Ramsey, I . . ."

Gerry tails off. Ramsey looks out the window. The train has started to slow down. He picks up his newspaper and places it back in his briefcase.

"Excuse me, Mr Baker, but this is my stop."

"Yes, Mr Ramsey, thank you for your time."

Ramsey sticks out his hand. Gerry takes it.

"Good luck, Mr Baker, but I don't think you'll need it."

Gerry isn't entirely sure what this means, but says: "Thank you, Mr Ramsey."

With that, Ramsey steps out of the compartment before alighting from the train. Gerry sits back down. He doesn't feel like re-joining his friends just yet. As the train resumes its journey, he curses under his breath. What right did he have to try to influence Alf Ramsey anyway? All he can do now is hope that the England manager makes the right decision.

Gerry Baker replays the conversation in his head, considers what he might have said if he'd had the courage of his convictions.

"Do I think my brother is the best?" he asks. "No, Mr Ramsey, I don't think my brother is the best . . . I know he is."

Afterword
by Nadia and Colin Baker

We always knew Dad was a great footballer but, during his lifetime, I don't think either of us fully appreciated just how special a player he was. To us, he was the man we could go to if we ever had a problem, he was the man of whom we were so, so proud and he's the man we have missed every day since his premature death in 2003. We always felt that his story, and that of our Uncle Gerry, was worthy of a book and, when Tom wrote to us in late 2011, the time just seemed right and we can't thank him enough for all his hard work. We are thrilled, as we know Dad would be, with the result. It serves as a fitting testimony to him, our mum and to Gerry's wife, Anne, who passed away in 2012. We love and miss you all.

Nadia and Colin Baker, February 2013

Club Career – Gerry Baker

Top flight unless otherwise stated

Chelsea

Season	League apps (goals)	FA Cup apps (goals)	League Cup* apps (goals)	Europe apps (goals)	Total apps (goals)
1955-56	n/a	n/a	1 (0)	n/a	1 (0)

*Southern Professional Floodlit Cup

Motherwell

Season	League apps (goals)	Scottish Cup apps (goals)	League Cup apps (goals)	Europe apps (goals)	Total apps (goals)
1956-57	2 (1)	n/a	n/a	n/a	2 (1)
1957-58	7 (3)	n/a	1 (0)	n/a	8 (3)
1958-59	n/a	n/a	1 (0)	n/a	1 (0)
Total	9 (4)	n/a	2 (0)	n/a	11 (4)

St Mirren

Season	League apps (goals)	Scottish Cup apps (goals)	League Cup apps (goals)	Europe apps (goals)	Total apps (goals)
1958-59	21 (20)	5 (8)	n/a	n/a	26 (28)
1959-60	33 (20)	4 (11)	6 (4)	n/a	43 (35)
1960-61	9 (2)	n/a	3 (1)	n/a	12 (3)
Total	63 (42)	9 (19)	9 (5)	n/a	81 (66)

Manchester City

Season	League apps (goals)	FA Cup apps (goals)	League Cup apps (goals)	Europe apps (goals)	Total apps (goals)
1960-61	22 (9)	1 (0)	1 (0)	n/a	24 (9)
1961-62	15 (5)	n/a	n/a	n/a	15 (5)
Total	37 (14)	1 (0)	1 (0)	n/a	39 (14)

Hibernian

Season	League apps (goals)	Scottish Cup apps (goals)	League Cup apps (goals)	Europe apps (goals)	Total apps (goals)
1961-62	21 (10)	2 (2)	n/a	n/a	23 (12)

1962-63	28 (13)	2 (0)	6 (4)	5 (3)	41 (20)
1963-64	10 (4)	n/a	9 (7)	n/a	19 (11)
Total	59 (27)	4 (2)	15 (11)	5 (3)	83 (43)

Ipswich Town

Season	League apps (goals)	FA Cup apps (goals)	League Cup apps (goals)	Europe apps (goals)	Total apps (goals)
1963-64 (Div 2)	21 (15)	2 (3)	n/a	n/a	23 (18)
1964-65	36 (16)	1 (0)	n/a	n/a	37 (16)
1965-66	38 (11)	2 (1)	3 (3)	n/a	43 (15)
1966-67	30 (13)	4 (0)	2 (1)	n/a	36 (14)
1967-68	11 (3)	n/a	2 (0)	n/a	13 (3)
Total	136 (58)	9 (4)	7 (4)	n/a	152 (66)

Coventry City

Season	League apps (goals)	FA Cup apps (goals)	League Cup apps (goals)	Europe apps (goals)	Total apps (goals)
1967-68	19 (4)	3 (1)	n/a	n/a	22 (5)
1968-69	11 (1)	n/a	n/a	n/a	11 (1)
1969-70	1 (0)	n/a	n/a	n/a	1 (0)
Total	31 (5)	3 (1)	n/a	n/a	34 (6)

Brentford (loan)

Season	League apps (goals)	FA Cup apps (goals)	League Cup apps (goals)	Europe apps (goals)	Total apps (goals)
(Div 4)					
1969-70	8 (2)	n/a	n/a	n/a	8 (2)

CAREER TOTAL

League	Cup	League Cup	Europe	Total
343 (152)	26 (26)	35 (20)	5 (3)	409 (201)

Club Career – Joe Baker

Top flight unless otherwise stated

Hibernian

Season	League apps (goals)	Scottish Cup apps (goals)	League Cup apps (goals)	Europe apps (goals)	Total apps (goals)
1957-58	25 (14)	7 (7)	1 (0)	n/a	33 (21)
1958-59	27 (25)	3 (0)	6 (5)	n/a	36 (30)
1959-60	33 (42)	3 (2)	6 (2)	n/a	42 (46)
1960-61	33 (21)	5 (11)	6 (6)	5 (6)	49 (44)
Total	118 (102)	18 (20)	19 (13)	5 (6)	160 (141)

Torino

Season	League apps (goals)	Coppa Italia apps (goals)		Europe apps (goals)	Total apps (goals)
1961-62	19 (7)	1 (0)		n/a	20 (7)

Arsenal

Season	League apps (goals)	FA Cup apps (goals)	League Cup apps (goals)	Europe apps (goals)	Total apps (goals)
1962-63	39 (29)	3 (2)	n/a	n/a	42 (31)
1963-64	39 (26)	4 (2)	n/a	2 (3)	45 (31)
1964-65	42 (25)	2 (0)	n/a	n/a	44 (25)
1965-66	24 (13)	1 (0)	n/a	n/a	25 (13)
Total	144 (93)	10 (4)	n/a	2 (3)	156 (100)

Nottingham Forest

Season	League apps (goals)	FA Cup apps (goals)	League Cup apps (goals)	Europe apps (goals)	Total apps (goals)
1965-66	14 (5)	n/a	n/a	n/a	14 (5)
1966-67	34 (16)	6 (3)	2 (0)	n/a	42 (19)
1967-68	39 (16)	2 (2)	2 (0)	4 (3)	47 (21)
1968-69	31 (4)	n/a	1 (0)	n/a	32 (4)
Total	118 (41)	8 (5)	5 (0)	4 (3)	135 (49)

Sunderland

Season	League apps (goals)	FA Cup apps (goals)	League Cup apps (goals)	Europe apps (goals)	Total apps (goals)
1969-70 (Div 2)	24 (2)	1 (0)	1 (0)	n/a	26 (2)
1970-71	16 (10)	1 (0)	1 (0)	n/a	18 (10)
Total	40 (12)	2 (0)	2 (0)	n/a	44 (12)

Hibernian

Season	League apps (goals)	Scottish Cup apps (goals)	League Cup apps (goals)	Europe apps (goals)	Total apps (goals)
1970-71	11 (8)	4 (0)	n/a	n/a	15 (8)
1971-72	11 (4)	3 (2)	5 (3)	n/a	19 (9)
Total	22 (12)	7 (2)	5 (3)	n/a	34 (17)

Raith Rovers

Season	League apps (goals)	Scottish Cup apps (goals)	League Cup apps (goals)	Europe apps (goals)	Total apps (goals)
(Div 2)					
1972-73	24 (25)	3 (1)	4 (1)	n/a	31 (27)
1973-74	25 (10)	3 (1)	7 (5)	n/a	35 (16)
Total	49 (35)	6 (2)	11 (6)	n/a	66 (43)

CAREER TOTAL

League	Cup	League Cup	Europe	Total
510 (302)	52 (33)	42 (25)	11 (12)	615 (372)

International Career – Gerry Baker

USA

7 appearances, 2 goals

1.
Date: 17 October 1968
Match type: World Cup qualifier, first round
Venue: Varsity Stadium, Toronto
Canada 4 United States 2 (Roy, Stritzl)
Attendance: 5,959

USA
G DeLong (Vancouver Royals)
H Kofler (NY Blau-Weiss Gottschee)
E Clear (St Louis Stars)
E Murphy (Chicago Mustangs)
N Krat (St Louis Stars)
A Bachmeier (Captain, Chicago Mustangs)
S Stritzl (NY Blau-Weiss Gottschee)
D Albrecht (Cleveland Stokers)
P Millar (NY Inter)
G Baker (Coventry City)
W Roy (Kansas City Spurs)

2.
Date: 20 October 1968
Match type: Friendly
Venue: Estadío Silvio Cator, Port-au-Prince, Haiti
Haiti 3 United States 6 (Millar 2, Albrecht 2, Roy 2)
Attendance: 7,284

USA
G DeLong (Vancouver Royals, replaced by V Gerley, NY Hungaria)

C Gentile (St Louis Stars)
E Clear (St Louis Stars)
E Murphy (Chicago Mustangs)
N Krat (St Louis Stars)
A Bachmeier (Captain, Chicago Mustangs)
S Stritzl (NY Blau-Weiss Gottschee)
D Albrecht (Cleveland Stokers)
P Millar (NY Inter, replaced by L Hausmann, Chicago Mustangs)
G Baker (Coventry City)
W Roy (Kansas City Spurs)

3.
Date: 23 October 1968
Match type: Friendly
Venue: Estadío Silvio Cator, Port-au-Prince, Haiti
Haiti 1 United States 0
Attendance: 5,641

USA
G DeLong (Vancouver Royals)
H Kofler (NY Blau-Weiss Gottschee)
N Krat (St Louis Stars)
C Gentile (St Louis Stars)
A Bachmeier (Captain, Chicago Mustangs)
G Tober (Cleveland Stokers)
L Hausmann, Chicago Mustangs
D Albrecht (Cleveland Stokers)
P Millar (NY Inter)
G Baker (Coventry City)
J Benedek (Houston Stars)

4.
Date: 27 October 1968
Match type: World Cup qualifier, first round
Venue: Fulton County Stadium, Atlanta
United States 1 (Albrecht) Canada 0
Attendance: 2,727

USA
S Feher (Kansas City Spurs)
R Gansler (Chicago Mustangs, replaced by E Clear, St Louis Stars)
N Krat (St Louis Stars)
C Gentile (St Louis Stars)
A Bachmeier (Captain, Chicago Mustangs)
E Murphy (Chicago Mustangs)
S Stritzl (NY Blau-Weiss Gottschee)
D Albrecht (Cleveland Stokers)
P Millar (NY Inter)
G Baker (Coventry City)
W Roy (Kansas City Spurs)

5.
Date: 2 November 1968
Match type: World Cup qualifier, first round
Venue: Municipal Stadium, Kansas City
United States 6 (Millar 3, Baker 2, Roy) Bermuda 2
Attendance: 2,265

USA
S Feher (Kansas City Spurs, replaced by G DeLong, Vancouver Royals)
R Gansler (Chicago Mustangs)
N Krat (St Louis Stars)
C Gentile (St Louis Stars)
A Bachmeier (Captain, Chicago Mustangs)
E Murphy (Chicago Mustangs)
S Stritzl (NY Blau-Weiss Gottschee)
D Albrecht (Cleveland Stokers)
P Millar (NY Inter)
G Baker (Coventry City)
W Roy (Kansas City Spurs)

6.
Date: 10 November 1968
Match type: World Cup qualifier, first round
Venue: National Stadium, Hamilton, Bermuda
Bermuda 0 United States 2 (Smith OG, Roy)
Attendance: 2,942

USA
G DeLong (Vancouver Royals)
C Gentile (St Louis Stars)
N Krat (St Louis Stars)
A Bachmeier (Captain, Chicago Mustangs)
J Benedek (Houston Stars)
E Murphy (Chicago Mustangs)
S Stritzl (NY Blau-Weiss Gottschee)
D Albrecht (Cleveland Stokers)
P Millar (NY Inter)
G Baker (Coventry City)
W Roy (Kansas City Spurs)

7.
Date: 11 May 1969
Match type: World Cup qualifier, semi-final
Venue: San Diego Stadium, San Diego
United States 0 Haiti 1
Attendance: 6,546

USA
O Banach (Chicago Hansa)
A Bachmeier (Chicago Kickers)
N Krat (Chicago Ukrainian Lions)
E Murphy (Chicago Maroons)
W Mata (LA Kickers)
S Stritzl (Baltimore Bays)
L Hausmann (St Louis Stars)
M Maliszewski (Baltimore Bays)
P Millar (Baltimore Bays)
G Baker (Coventry City)
D Albrecht (Baltimore Bays)

International Career – Joe Baker

Scotland Schoolboys

2 appearances, 3 goals

1.
Date: 7 May 1955
Match type: Victory Shield
Venue: Somerset Park, Ayr
Scotland Schoolboys 5 (Reid 2, Hunter, Baker, Burns) Wales Schoolboys 2
Attendance: 7,000

Scotland Schoolboys
J McDonald (Dundee)
J McGregor (Larbert)
D Leiper (Motherwell and Wishaw)
W Stevenson (Edinburgh)
W Cook (Captain, Kilmarnock)
J McNab (Stirlingshire)
W Little (Dumfries)
S Reid (Motherwell and Wishaw)
J Baker (Motherwell and Wishaw)
J Hunter (Coatbridge and Airdrie)
R Burns (Govan)

2.
Date: 14 May 1955
Match type: Victory Shield
Venue: Goodison Park, Liverpool
England Schoolboys 2 Scotland Schoolboys 2 (Baker 2)
Attendance: 37,499

Scotland Schoolboys
J Neason (Cambuslang)
A Goldie (Ayrshire East)
D Leiper (Motherwell and Wishaw)
W Stevenson (Edinburgh)
W Cook (Captain, Kilmarnock)
J McNab (Stirlingshire)
M Bogie (Edinburgh)
S Reid (Motherwell and Wishaw)
J Baker (Motherwell and Wishaw)
J Hunter (Coatbridge and Airdrie)
R Burns (Govan)

England Under-23s

5 appearances, 4 goals

1.
Date: 24 September 1958
Match type: Friendly
Venue: Hillsborough, Sheffield
England Under-23s 4 (Charlton 3, Greaves) Poland Under-23s 1
Attendance: 38,525

England U23s
A Hodgkinson (Sheffield United)

J Armfield (Captain, Blackpool)
A Allen (Stoke City)
M Setters (West Bromwich Albion)
M Scott (Chelsea)
W McGuinness (Manchester United)
P Brabrook (Chelsea)
J Greaves (Chelsea)
J Baker (Hibernian)
R Charlton (Manchester United)
A Scanlon (Manchester United)

2.

Date: 15 October 1958
Match type: Friendly
Venue: Carrow Road, Norwich
England Under-23s 3 (Charlton 2, Greaves) Czechoslovakia Under-23s 0
Attendance: 38,000

England U23s

A Hodgkinson (Sheffield United)
J Armfield (Captain, Blackpool)
A Allen (Stoke City)
M Setters (West Bromwich Albion)
M Scott (Chelsea)
W McGuinness (Manchester United)
P Brabrook (Chelsea)
J Greaves (Chelsea)
J Baker (Hibernian)
R Charlton (Manchester United)
A Scanlon (Manchester United)

3.

Date: 11 November 1959
Match type: Friendly
Venue: Roker Park, Sunderland
England Under-23s 2 (Baker, Crowe) France Under-23s 0
Attendance: 26,495

England U23s

A Macedo (Fulham Athletic)
G Cohen (Fulham Athletic)
M McNeil (Middlesbrough)
M Setters (Captain, West Bromwich Albion)
P Swan (Sheffield Wednesday)
J Smith (West Ham United)
C Crowe (Leeds United)
P Dobing (Blackburn Rovers)
J Baker (Hibernian)
G Eastham (Newcastle United)
J Sydenham (Southampton)

4.

Date: 16 March 1960
Match type: Friendly, Hillsborough, Sheffield
England Under-23s 5 (Eastham pen, Greaves, Baker 2, Paine) Netherlands Under-23s 2
Attendance: 21,163

England U23s

A Macedo (Fulham Athletic)
G Cohen (Fulham Athletic)
M McNeil (Middlesbrough)
M Setters (Captain, Manchester United)
P Swan (Sheffield Wednesday)
A Kay (Sheffield Wednesday)
T Paine (Southampton)
G Eastham (Newcastle United)
J Baker (Hibernian)
J Greaves (Chelsea)
E Holliday (Middlesbrough)

5.

Date: 2 November 1960
Match type: Friendly
Venue: St James' Park, Newcastle
England Under-23s 1 (Baker) Italy Under-23s 1
Attendance: 15,064

England U23s

A Macedo (Fulham Athletic)
J Angus (Captain, Burnley)
M McNeil (Middlesbrough)
A Mullery (Fulham Athletic)
B Labone (Everton)
R Moore (West Ham United)
J Connelly (Burnley)
P Dobing (Blackburn Rovers)
J Baker (Hibernian)
J Fantham (Sheffield Wednesday)
R Charlton (Manchester United)

England

8 appearances, 3 goals

1.
Date: 18 November 1959
Match type: Home Championship
Venue: Wembley Stadium, London
England 2 (Baker, Parry) Northern
   Ireland 1
Attendance: 60,000

England
R Springett (Sheffield Wednesday)
D Howe (West Bromwich Albion)
A Allen (Stoke City)
R Clayton (Captain, Blackburn Rovers)
K Brown (West Ham United)
R Flowers (Wolverhampton Wanderers)
J Connelly (Burnley)
J Haynes (Fulham Athletic)
J Baker (Hibernian)
R Parry (Bolton Wanderers)
E Holliday (Middlesbrough)

2.
Date: 19 April 1960
Match type: Home Championship
Venue: Hampden Park, Glasgow
Scotland 1 England 1 (Charlton pen)
Attendance: 129,783

England
R Springett (Sheffield Wednesday)
J Armfield (Blackpool)
R Wilson (Huddersfield Town)
R Clayton (Captain, Blackburn Rovers)
W Slater (Wolverhampton Wanderers)
R Flowers (Wolverhampton Wanderers)
J Connelly (Burnley)
P Broadbent (Wolverhampton
   Wanderers)
J Baker (Hibernian)
R Parry (Bolton Wanderers)
R Charlton (Manchester United)

3.
Date: 11 May 1960
Match type: Friendly
Venue: Wembley Stadium, London
England 3 (Douglas, Greaves, Haynes)
   Yugoslavia 3
Attendance: 60,000

England
R Springett (Sheffield Wednesday)
J Armfield (Blackpool)
R Wilson (Huddersfield Town)
R Clayton (Captain, Blackburn Rovers)
P Swan (Sheffield Wednesday)
R Flowers (Wolverhampton Wanderers)
B Douglas (Blackburn Rovers)
J Haynes (Captain, Fulham Athletic)
J Baker (Hibernian)
J Greaves (Chelsea)
R Charlton (Manchester United)

4.
Date: 15 May 1960
Match type: Friendly
Venue: Estadio Santiago Bernabeu,
   Madrid
Spain 3 England 0
Attendance: 77,000

England
R Springett (Sheffield Wednesday)
J Armfield (Blackpool)
R Wilson (Huddersfield Town)
R Robson (West Bromwich Albion)
P Swan (Sheffield Wednesday)
R Flowers (Wolverhampton Wanderers)
P Brabrook (Chelsea)
J Haynes (Captain, Fulham Athletic)
J Baker (Hibernian)
J Greaves (Chelsea)
R Charlton (Manchester United)

5.
Date: 22 May 1960
Match type: Friendly
Venue: Nepstadion, Budapest
Hungary 2 England 0
Attendance: 90,000

England
R Springett (Sheffield Wednesday)
J Armfield (Blackpool)
R Wilson (Huddersfield Town)
R Robson (West Bromwich Albion)
P Swan (Sheffield Wednesday)
R Flowers (Wolverhampton Wanderers)
B Douglas (Blackburn Rovers)
J Haynes (Captain, Fulham Athletic)
J Baker (Hibernian)
D Viollet (Manchester United)
R Charlton (Manchester United)

6.
Date: 10 November 1965
Match type: Home Championship
Venue: Wembley Stadium, London
England 2 (Baker, Peacock) Northern
   Ireland 1
Attendance: 70,000

England
G Banks (Leicester City)
G Cohen (Fulham Athletic)
R Wilson (Everton)
N Stiles (Manchester United)
J Charlton (Leeds United)
R Moore (Captain, West Ham United)
P Thompson (Liverpool)
J Baker (Arsenal)
A Peacock (Leeds United)
J Connelly (Manchester United)
R Charlton (Manchester United)

7.
Date: 8 December 1965
Match type: Friendly
Venue: Estadio Santiago Bernabeu,
   Madrid

Spain 0 England 2 (Baker, Hunt)
Attendance: 30,000

England
G Banks (Leicester City)
G Cohen (Fulham Athletic)
R Wilson (Everton)
N Stiles (Manchester United)
J Charlton (Leeds United)
R Moore (Captain, West Ham United)
A Ball (Blackpool)
J Baker (Arsenal, replaced by N Hunter,
   Leeds United, 35 minutes)
R Hunt (Liverpool)
G Eastham (Arsenal)
   R Charlton (Manchester United)

8.
Date: 5 January 1966
Match type: Friendly
Venue: Goodison Park, Liverpool
England 1 (Moore) Poland 1
Attendance: 47,839

England
G Banks (Leicester City)
G Cohen (Fulham Athletic)
R Wilson (Everton)
N Stiles (Manchester United)
J Charlton (Leeds United)
R Moore (Captain, West Ham United)
A Ball (Blackpool)
R Hunt (Liverpool)
J Baker (Arsenal)
G Eastham (Arsenal)
G Harris (Burnley)

Other England matches

3 appearances, 3 goals

1.
Date: 6 May 1960
Match type: Inter-level international
Venue: Highbury, London

England 2 (Baker 2) Young England 1

England
R Springett (Sheffield Wednesday)
J Armfield (Blackpool)
R Wilson (Huddersfield Town)
R Robson (West Bromwich Albion)
P Swan (Sheffield Wednesday)
T Kay (Sheffield Wednesday)
P Brabrook (Chelsea)
J Haynes (Captain, Fulham Athletic)
J Baker (Hibernian)
J Greaves (Chelsea)
R Charlton (Manchester United)

2.
Date: 21 September 1960
Match type: Friendly (unofficial)
Venue: Maine Road, Manchester
England Under-23s 5 (Baker, Charlton
    2, Moore, Paine) Veije BK (Denmark)
    1

England U23s
G Banks (Leicester City)
J Angus (Burnley)
M McNeil (Middlesbrough)

M Barber (Barnsley)
B Labone (Everton)
R Moore (West Ham United)
T Paine (Southampton)
F Hill (Bolton Wanderers)
J Baker (Hibernian)
D Burnside (West Bromwich Albion)
R Charlton (Manchester United)

3.
Date: 5 May 1961
Match type: Inter-level international
Venue: Stamford Bridge, London
England 1 Young England 1 (Robson)

Young England
A Macedo (Fulham Athletic)
J Angus (Captain, Burnley)
L Ashurst (Sunderland)
J Kirkham (Wolverhampton Wanderers)
J McGrath (Newcastle United)
R Moore (West Ham United)
T Paine (Southampton)
F Hill (Bolton Wanderers)
J Baker (Hibernian)
J Robson (Burnley)
G Harris (Burnley)

Baker versus Baker

22 November 1958, Scottish First Division
St Mirren 2 (Campbell, **Gerry Baker**) Hibernian 1 (Aitken)

7 November 1959, Scottish First Division
St Mirren 2 (Bryceland, Gemmell) Hibernian 3 (Preston, Johnstone, **Joe Baker**)

29 October 1960, Scottish First Division
Hibernian 4 (Kinloch 3, Ormond) St Mirren 3 (**Gerry Baker**, Miller, Frye)

11 October 1961, friendly
Manchester City 4 (Dobing, Kennedy, Hayes, **Gerry Baker**) Torino 3 (**Joe Baker 3**)

18 February 1964, English First Division
Ipswich Town 1 (**Gerry Baker**) Arsenal 2 (Eastham, Strong)

Gerry Baker – 4 goals
Joe Baker – 4 goals

Bibliography

Allaway, Roger, Jose, Colin and Litterer, David, *The Encyclopedia of American Soccer History* (Scarecrow Press, 2001)

Allaway, Roger and Jose, Colin, *The United States Tackles the World Cup* (second edition, St Johann Press, 2011)

Attaway, Pete, *Nottingham Forest – A Complete Record 1865-1991* (Breedon Books, 1991)

Bowler, Dave, *Winning Isn't Everything – A Biography of Alf Ramsey* (Orion, 1992)

Brown, Jim, *Coventry City, The Elite Era – A Complete Record 1967-2001* (Desert Island Books, 2004)

Cirino, Tony, *US Soccer vs the World* (Damon Press, 1983)

Charlton, Sir Bobby, *The Autobiography – My England Years* (Headline, 2008)

Clough, Brian, *Cloughie: Walking on Water – My Life* (Headline, 2002)

Fabian, A.H. and Green, Geoffrey (editors), *Association Football, Volume Two* (Caxton Publishing, 1960)

Fabian, A.H. and Green, Geoffrey (editors), *Association Football, Volume Four* (Caxton Publishing, 1960)

Foot, John, *Calcio – A History of Italian Football* (Harper Perennial, 2007)

Giller, Norman, *Billy Wright – A Hero for All Seasons* (Robson Books, 2002)

Goodwin, Bob, *The Pride of North London* (Polar Print Group, 1997)

Greaves, Jimmy, *Greavsie – The Autobiography* (Time Warner, 2003)

Greaves, Jimmy and Giller, Norman, *The Sixties Revisited* (Queen Anne Press, 1992)

Hurst, Geoff, *1966 and All That* (Headline, 2002)

Inglis, Simon (editor), *The Best of Charles Buchan's Football Monthly, September 1951–August 1971* (English Heritage and Football Monthly Ltd, 2006)

Jeffrey, Jim and Fry, Genge, *The Men Who Made Motherwell Football Club* (Tempus Publishing, 2001)

Law, Denis, *The King* (Bantam Press, 2003)

Litster, John, *Always Next Season – 125 years of Raith Rovers Football Club* (Programme Monthly, 2008)

McColl, Graham, *England – The Alf Ramsey Years* (Chameleon Books, 1998)

McKinstry, Leo, *Jack & Bobby – A Story of Brothers in Conflict* (Collins Willow, 2003)

McKinstry, Leo, *Sir Alf* (HarperSport, 2007)

McLintock, Frank, *True Grit* (Headline, 2005)

McVay, David, *Forest's Cult Heroes* (Know the Score Books, 2007)

Milburn, Jack, *Jackie Milburn – A Man of Two Halves* (Mainstream Publishing, 2003)

Paterson, Jack and McPherson, Bob, *Marching On – 125 years of the St Mirren Football Club* (Saltire Graphics, 2005)

Reilly, Lawrie, *The Life and Times of Last Minute Reilly* (Black & White Publishing, 2010)

Scott, Brian, *The Terrible Trio* (Sportsprint Publishing, 1990)

Soar, Phil and Tyler, Martin, *Arsenal – The Official Illustrated History 1886-2010* (Hamlyn, 2010)

Spurling, Jon, *Rebels for the Cause – The Alternative History of Arsenal Football Club* (Mainstream Publishing, 2004)

Stennett, Ceri, *As Good as It Gets* (Stennett Books, 2011)

Stiles, Nobby, *After the Ball – My Autobiography* (Hodder & Stoughton, 2003)

St John, Ian, *The Saint – My Autobiography* (Hodder & Stoughton, 2005)

Wangerin, David, *Soccer in a Football World* (WSC Books Ltd, 2006)

Wilson, Bob, *Behind the Network* (Hodder & Stoughton, 2003)

Other publications:

The Arizona Republic, The Bulletin, Charles Buchan's Football Monthly, The Daily Express, The Daily Mail, The Daily Mirror, The Daily Record, The Daily Star, The Dumfries and Galloway Standard, The Edinburgh Evening News, The Evening Citizen, The Evening Dispatch, The Falkirk Herald, The Glasgow Evening Times, The Guardian, The Herald, La Stampa, The Motherwell Times, The News of the World, The Nottingham Evening Post, The Paisley Daily Express, The People, Scotland on Sunday, The Scotsman, The Sun, The Sunday Herald, The Sunday Post, The Sunderland Echo, The Telegraph, The Times, The Topical Times Football Book, The Wishaw Press

Other sources:

BBC Radio Five Live, BBC Radio Scotland, BBC *Match of the Day*; Websites: bbc.co.uk, bluemoonmcfc.co.uk, britishpathe.com, englandfootballonline.com, fitbastats.com, rsssf.com, stmirren.info, thestatcat.co.uk